FREE

FROM THE

CAGE

Liberate Yourself from Negative Feelings and
Create Powerful, Lasting Mindset Changes

FREE
FROM THE
CAGE

A Guide to Take You from
Overwhelmed to Peace

JENNIFER RIGGS

For information contact:

_____

Published by:
J.T.F. Publishing

Cover design by Klassic Designs
Interior book design by Francine Platt, Eden Graphics, Inc.

Paperback 978-1-958626-94-8
eBook 978-1-958626-95-5
Audio 978-1-958626-96-2

Library of Congress Number: 2024907137

Manufactured in the United States of America

First Edition

For everyone in need of healing.
Keep going.

TABLE OF CONTENTS

A NOTE FROM THE AUTHOR:

Someone asked me once if I was going to write my autobiography, what would I call it? It didn't take much time to respond with Work in Progress. While this is not an autobiography, and it's not called Work in Progress, it felt important for me to share this. I believe I am a work in progress, and in fact we all are. Life is about progressing and learning about who we are and how we can be the best, most authentic version of ourselves we can be.

I've been doing various energy work and emotional processing with clients for over a decade. In that time, I've learned a lot not only about myself and my own parts in need of introspection and change to move my progress along, but have seen similarities and patterns among those who have asked me to join them on their healing journey. Within these pages I'll share the knowledge and understanding I have gained as well as positive and lasting outcomes for myself and my clients.

Free from the Cage

Liberate Yourself from Negative Feelings and
Create Powerful, Lasting Mindset Changes

Introduction

Last December, I got all new lights for our Christmas tree. I was so happy with the results of the fresh, bright, and warm LED lights and how nice the tree looked. It was beautiful. The lights we had previously used had random bulbs burned out and even whole sections of lights weren't working. These new lights were just perfect. One afternoon, I was hurrying to tidy up before guests came over and plugged my vacuum into the same outlet the lights were connected to. As I flipped the vacuum on, the entire tree went dark. "Nooo!" I gasped. Then I thought "no problem" I must have tripped a breaker. A quick run to the basement to check the box, and surely, I could fix it. But no, this was not the case.

Dark. The lights were all totally dark. I clearly over-loaded the strands and completely destroyed them. Using this example, think of each light on the strands as an emotion. We are all likely walking around carrying a variety of stored emotions such as anger, sadness, guilt, shame, grief, unworthiness, and more. This concoction often shows up as a more encompassing feeling of overwhelm. The longer we avoid dealing with each feeling, the greater chance we have to overload our physical and emotional systems.

The overwhelm demands our attention, but we avoid it by working too hard, exercising too much, playing video games nonstop, drinking alcohol to excess, shopping compulsively, gambling beyond our means, eating too much or too little, or even endlessly scrolling social media. You name the fixation that keeps you busy and avoiding acknowledging your feelings, and you might start to see where you are desperately trying to contain, compartmentalize, and control your emotions.

As the electrical system surged on my Christmas lights, we can compare this to the intensity the demands of life bring us, and how our feelings push to get out as we push to avoid them in an effort to just keep going. However, as with the lights on my tree, at some point we are likely to reach a breaking point when the surge is too strong, and everything comes to a stop.

The word "overwhelm" is defined by Merriam-Webster as:

Overwhelm (verb) to upset or overthrow.
Cover completely: Submerge
Overcome by superior force or numbers
To overpower in thought or feeling

Reading this definition, do you often find yourself overwhelmed?

Have you been overwhelmed this month?

This week?

Today?

If so, you are not alone. If you asked these questions to almost anyone you meet, you will likely hear a "yes." This is an all-too-common theme in our fast paced, demanding world. There is so much emphasis on doing more that we forget we have limits, and we get so caught up in striving we don't take care of our emotional needs nearly enough.

Many of the blocks we have to our success and happiness are the result of the overwhelm our unprocessed emotions create. The problem is we are often unaware they even exist. We go along in life with a smile on our face and just keep moving through our days. It will often take something big to get our attention and prompt us to do something to work with those feelings. Sometimes it will even take something catastrophic to make us uncomfortable enough to do it because we get so used to avoiding what we feel it just seems normal to be this way. It might be a serious health problem, a major loss, or life change we were not expecting that will incite the overwhelm when one too many feelings is added to our subconscious storage system of emotions. This is very often the point when people will seek change. Comparing it to the lights on my tree, the surge from the major event pushes us to take action.

Conversely, the overwhelm you may be carrying could be making you feel unable to make changes in your life. You might feel paralyzed to be any different than you currently are, but at the same time, you may be wanting the change so badly yet find yourself powerless to make it happen. Imagine a bird in a cage. There is limited space for the bird to fly around in. She can only go as far as the bars of her environment allow.

She might fly up against those bars, and even be able to see the sky above her, but unless the door is opened, she is resigned to remaining within the space she has been given.

We sometimes create cages for ourselves just like the bird must endure. Those cages are built from our unprocessed emotions that are contained in the overwhelm. The bars of fear, sadness, grief, confusion, anxiety, anger, non-forgiveness, and more close in on us and make our world smaller. They inhibit our ability to see other options that allow us to grow as individuals. The tendency to continually relive painful experiences compounds the negative feelings, and the bars become stronger.

There's a better way. There's a path to opening the door to the virtual cage of your overwhelming negative feelings. A path to finding happiness, authenticity, and freedom, and when this path is followed, the overload or paralysis to your system can be avoided.

The word healing is thrown around a lot these days—I admit, I do it too. It seems to be some kind of all-encompassing word for getting your life together. Which is probably pretty true. To me, healing means looking inward, while examining the painful experiences in your life, processing your emotions about them, and integrating what you have learned from those experiences so that you can make positive changes to create a better future for yourself.

What does it mean to "process" your emotions? Well, it means that instead of pushing emotions down or away, you acknowledge them, you experience them, and you gain understanding from them. We feel things for a reason. It's not random. We feel things because events in our lives create these energetic charges within us. Sadly, we so often believe it's better to ignore our feelings than go through the messiness of receiving the insight they are there to bring us. However, the more we ignore feelings, the more difficult life gets, and the smaller our cage becomes.

The first thing we need to move toward our freedom is have an awareness we are not really living the life we want, and a solid willingness to transform. When I say not living the life we want, this can mean a wide range of things from being in the wrong career, relationship, home, friendships, habits, or really anything. If we are feeling like something is off in our lives, it probably is. The key aspect to helping you find clarity about what you truly want is to feel your feelings.

The goal of this book is to help you recognize the feelings you need to explore and experience to begin to make powerful mindset changes so that you can reach your goals and your true potential, and above all that, to become your best and most authentic self. It's broken down into two parts. Part I is about accessing your subconscious mind to effectively process your emotions. I'll explain why this is so critical as well as ways to begin this journey. Part II will talk about mindset changes that can be made via the power of your emotional releasing and integrating.

Your subconscious mind holds all of the answers to all of the questions you have. It's the secret keeper in your life. The secrets to healing your personal world, the secrets to letting go, the secrets to your dreams, desires, and most importantly, to your true self. The main secret contained in the subconscious is all of your emotions. The subconscious remembers our feelings from events of our past and stores them. When we don't actually feel them, that's when trouble begins. When we process our feelings, it's like opening a hidden door to clarity. The answers are there, under the feelings. The really wonderful thing about your subconscious mind is even though it sounds mysterious, it's easy enough to access, and once you do, so many things in your life will improve.

The subconscious also has a unique way of knowing what it is you need to pay attention to most, and those things will jump out at you first. For example, if setting boundaries is something you've been struggling with, that chapter will probably resonate most with you, while something you've worked on in the past you may move through quickly without grabbing onto much. That being said, if you read this again at another time, something new may draw your attention.

When you address the overwhelm and feel your feelings, your truth becomes evident and attainable. When you process what you feel, you can the change the way you think. Your new life is waiting for you right there, outside the cage of emotional confinement. Get ready to turn your key.

PART I

Feel Your Feelings, Find Your Freedom

CHAPTER 1

YOUR INNER NAVIGATOR

Quiet the mind and the soul will speak.

~ Ma Jaya Sati Bhagavati, The 11 Karmic Spaces

We were all born with our own internal navigation system, and when we learn how to connect to it, the path of our lives becomes much easier to travel, just like knowing where to turn when we are finding our way to a new location. That inner navigation system is our subconscious mind. This is where our feelings, memories, values, our view of ourselves and the world around us are stored. The subconscious does things automatically, like driving home from work or to the store. We don't have to think about it after doing it many times, we just know how to get there without planning or scripting, it's already programmed into our mind through previous repetitions. It also allows us to do things like riding a bike or anything we've learned and can repeat with ease.

In contrast, our conscious mind is where logical thought happens, where we can do things like math or follow directions. It's where anything we are currently thinking about happens. It analyzes and plans. The conscious mind is our "thinking" mind, and our subconscious is our "feeling" mind. The subconscious mind makes up for about 95 percent of our brain use. It's powerful and emotion driven. Our feelings can (and often do) overpower our thoughts.

Not only do we repeat behaviors over and over out of subconscious programming, but we also repeat emotions we have had over and over. For example, imagine that as a child, something happened that really scared you. It's likely when that fear occurred you didn't know how to process it or understand what was happening. It's also possible you didn't have an adult helping you through it either. It may have been because you didn't tell an adult, or perhaps any adults around you didn't realize how much you were affected, or in some cases, the adult(s) around you may have created the fear.

That fear gets stored in your subconscious mind and leaves an imprint. Then if you experience fear again at a later time and it isn't processed, it is added to the first fearful feeling. So, for the sake of creating an image, imagine fear number one is a bar on a cage. If you get frightened again, another bar goes in place. With each subsequent fearful event that is not properly processed in the moment, a new bar is added. The more fears that show up, the more bars appear, and the more locked down we become. It may be increasingly difficult to do certain things or go places that might trigger the fear. It may be challenging to interact with people who either played a part in the fear or remind us of them. The bars, or fears become limiting as those negative emotions get stored in the body and mind. The limitations and negative effects may grow and grow, and a stuck or trapped feeling occurs as a cage is built around us.

At this point, we may be feeling like we have no options because all we can see are the bars of the cage, holding us in. In an odd way it might feel protective, but in the end, we are only being held prisoner to a negative emotion we are reluctant to face.

In my hypnotherapy practice, when clients come to me, they frequently don't really know what exactly is wrong, they just know something is making them uncomfortable. The discomfort can come from emotional distress like anxiety, sadness, overwhelm with life, and so much more. It can also show up in physical pain which I will talk about in depth in a future chapter, but so often it will be both emotional and physical leading them to a point of not only wanting a change, but really, truly needing one.

Breaking free of the cages we create for ourselves can be made so much easier when we learn how to connect to our subconscious and really investigate as well as process through our feelings about situations in our lives. Tapping into our subconscious mind enables us to move closer to what is the right thing for us and further from what we do out of habit.

So often we are on autopilot, not only when it comes to driving home after a long day of work, but we are on autopilot repeating the same behaviors day after day, even if we want a different outcome. We tend to lean into the familiar. We reach for what we know because it makes us feel comfortable even when that comfort is, believe it or not, uncomfortable.

How can something that is comfortable be uncomfortable?

Well, when we know what to expect, we cling to that. We may not like the results we get, but we know all about how to get there, and so it's like we keep on driving down the same old bumpy road that throws stones on our car and leaves a coating of dust.

Breaking that habit requires doing something new. Anything. Just changing something up can begin to make a shift for us. Drive down a different road and see if it's paved. Is the sun shining there? Maybe it takes you to a brand-new place you've never been. The possibilities are endless, we just have to be willing to take the risk.

For example, if you want to get in shape, but continually say you don't have time, yet every morning you spend thirty minutes on social media. Instead of doing that, you hop on an elliptical at the gym or go for a walk, soon enough, you will begin to feel differently. You might lose a few pounds, which might inspire you to add another change. Maybe then you start to take a walk on your lunch break to a park to eat a packed lunch instead of grabbing fast food. You might find you not only are losing weight, but you are saving money. You might find you are happier not seeing so much social media. You might find you desire MORE changes. Maybe next you decide to take a class doing something you've always been interested in. Maybe in that class you meet your new best friend. Maybe that new best friend has a brother who you fall in love with, get married, buy a house, and have children with. Look what happens when you start to change just one small thing!

All right, is it likely that all these wonderful things happen just because you start taking a walk in the morning? Maybe not, but guess what? You won't know if you continue to start your day looking at your phone and scrolling through social media. It only takes one action to make a change. The more changes you make, the braver you will become, and the more opportunities will present themselves to you.

When we have an experience, there are emotions involved, and when those emotions are not fully felt or processed, we may push them down and pretend like they don't exist. We can pretend until the next time something triggers that old feeling and then boom; it all comes rushing back. Now we've added another experience to it, and the bad feeling from before is now bigger. This is another illustration of the bars of the cage.

This will continue on over the years until we address the feeling for real and let ourselves truly FEEL it. After years of working with people and helping them sort things out in their subconscious mind, I've learned while we may all have different experiences, we all have the same emotions. It's all relative, what one person views as tragic another person may view as not a big deal, and vice versa. It doesn't make one person's experiences more or less than another's. The emotions carry the same weight. So many of us struggle with not feeling good enough. Actually, I don't think I've ever worked with a person that has not cited this as an issue at some point.

Why is that? Well, the tendency to look for worth outside of ourselves is huge. We seek validation through achievement, praise, and acceptance from others. The truth is, though, this is not at all where our worth lies. Later on in this book, I will talk about self-worth and self-love and how we can begin to see where it REALLY is.

So, what is it that guides and directs us through life when we are bombarded with messages about what is "good," what is "bad," and what we should and shouldn't do almost constantly? Fortunately, we come with built-in navigation tools, sometimes we just need to learn how to use them. We do know what is right for us in any situation, even when we think we don't. Therein lies the problem, "thinking we know." Our subconscious is the one with the real answer, the truth that fits who we are and what we believe exists there, and getting those answers comes through asking ourselves what we feel about something...not what we think about it. We can rationalize and talk ourselves into or out of anything, but there comes a price with that. When we are not being true to ourselves and what is really best for us, there are many different negative consequences, such as anxiety, depression, pain, and general unhappiness to name a few.

Have you ever had your washing machine go off-balance? When the clothes are not positioned in a way that keeps the machine rotating in a consistent way, it will rattle loudly while shaking like the walls of your house are coming down. It will disrupt the washing cycle and likely give you an error code. When our emotions are not processed, we get thrown off-balance too. We may become stressed, overwhelmed, and anxious, or our body may start feeling off with headaches, stomachaches, or back pain. In essence, our physical body is giving us the equivalent of the washing machine error code.

When your washer starts shaking like an earthquake has hit, do you run to the machine to quickly open the lid to quiet it? I know I do. Do you reach inside and begin pulling out heavy items and try to decide how to get things spinning properly again? What if you gave that same attention to yourself, and to your emotions? If when you felt off-balance, you took action with the same speed as correcting the banging of your washing machine?

Too often though, we act like nothing is wrong and like we can just go on doing things as we were before, and it will magically change or improve. Sadly, this is not the case. Nothing ever really just resolves itself, does it? At least not entirely. A situation may change because of an outside influence or another person's decision, but there will always be feelings associated with that change that at some point will need to be examined and felt. For example, a relationship may be difficult, and you may not know what to do about it, and while you are avoiding making a change, the other person may end up deciding they are going to leave, or they no longer want to be friends. Suddenly, the relationship you were so unhappy with now has you asking, "What did I do wrong?" Those feelings still need to be processed, or it may set us up for feeling like in future relationships the other person may leave or in a friendship we are doing something wrong, even if we are not. Our emotional experiences leave an imprint on our subconscious mind, and we begin to believe history will repeat itself if we haven't worked through traumatic events we have experienced.

So, how do we get to a place where we doubt our worth,

find ourselves anxious, stressed, afraid, and lost in the first place? A few different factors come into play here. As I said, some of it comes from our personal life experiences, but the greater majority of it comes from what we have learned from our family and the way they have always done things. This is not to blame anyone, because ultimately, we are responsible for our own healing, or lack of it.

John Mayer has a song called "In the Blood," and the lines of the song always strike a chord in me to question where our behaviors and beliefs come from. The lyrics ask if the way our parents are, is how we are also destined to be, and if what we have witnessed in our upbringing holds us to unchangeable patterns. While we do take most of our behaviors and view of ourselves and the world and the way we approach life from our parents, I also think as John questions, what is in our blood, so to speak, is not something we are forced to keep forever. I truly believe it only takes one person to break a pattern of behaviors or familial conditioning. We may find ourselves with traits similar to our parents, but that doesn't mean we have to keep them any more than they have to. We DO have choices about how we live, what we believe about ourselves and the society we live in. It's up to us to decide what we keep and what we dispense with.

The things we observe and pick up from our family are the biggest part of how we become who we are. The world all around us impacts us, there is no way around that, but for the most part what we learn from our family of origin is what we take into the world. Our interactions with others, what we observe, and the traumas we are faced with also play a part in who we become, but mostly from a standpoint of our response to them, which was programmed in us at the time of birth. There will be good and bad from all those things. The bad may plague us for a while, but we have the option to work through those events, to question them, and in the end, change anything that just isn't working for us. Our experiences and interactions serve to help create the person we ultimately were meant to be. All those feelings, views, and ideas are right there in our subconscious mind, waiting for us to question, to challenge, and to change if necessary.

When working with hypnosis clients, I tell them I am not going to be putting them into a trance, but rather taking them out of their trance. We are all in a "trance" of sorts following whatever beliefs and patterns we have been going along with throughout our lives, repeating old ways and old programming. We stay in that trance until we decide what we are doing hurts more than venturing off to new territory.

Circling back to my view of healing, I think maybe there is a different word for this process of emotional integration than healing. I do think we are healed through our life experiences, but perhaps we are also born through them. Perhaps we are becoming with each and every tear and heartbreak, with every difficult relationship, missed opportunity, and challenge on our path. Maybe we are all really just being born every day as we get closer and closer to who we really are.

If you are reading this and find yourself saying yes, something isn't working in my life, but I just don't know what it is, checking in with your subconscious can help you find those answers. It's difficult to change something if you really don't know what it is that needs changing. The navigator in your subconscious mind knows though. The answers are there. Let's go get them.

KEY FOR CHANGE

Spend some quiet time noticing cues you may have that let you know you are not in alignment.

If you are experiencing anxiety, sadness, overwhelm or recurrent pain frequently, these may be good indicators you have some unprocessed negative emotions in your energetic system.

Some questions to consider:

- Are there events or people that trigger negative feelings for you?

- How do you feel about yourself?

- What are some things you would like to feel or behave differently about?

- Do you think that behaviors you have are unchangeable?

Keep those cues and thoughts in mind as you move through the chapters and exercises in this book. It might be helpful to start a journal for the processes I will share with you.

Knock on the Door to Your Subconscious

So, how do we access this mysterious subconscious mind that has all the answers? One way is through hypnotherapy, which is an excellent way to reach your inner mind. To use this method, it will be best to consult a certified practitioner.

The process of regression which involves going back to past events via your subconscious mind brings up and allows you to resolve unprocessed emotions as well as finding your true feelings about things.

What about when you are at home, on your own? First, let's talk about what truth feels like in your body. This is important, because again, we can talk ourselves into or out of anything, but if we really start to pay attention to physical sensations along with messages we receive in our mind, we can easily know the real answer to our questions. This can become a wonderful way for you to respect your feelings, and when you respect your feelings, you can work your way through them.

Here's an exercise to help you learn what physical sensations come along with truth for you. Make a statement you know to be true, for example, if you love ice cream, say, "I love ice cream, it's my favorite food" (or insert favorite food of your choice). As you say it, pay attention to how the words come out of your mouth. Do they come easily? Do you feel like you are holding anything back? Also notice what your body feels like, is there any place you feel any resistance when saying this?

Now, say a statement you know to be false like "I'll never eat ice cream again, I hate it" and notice the same things, does this statement come easily? Does your body seem to resist it? You can try this also by saying your name "My name is (insert your name)" and then use a name that is not your own and say it again. Notice what feels true and what does not. Saying your name is something other than your own may make you laugh, or you might feel like your mouth clenches especially if you use a name of someone you dislike.

You'll feel a flow and ease with truthful statements.

This applies to everything. So, if you've been invited to something and you are not sure you want to attend, instead of trying to rationalize all the why you should and why you should nots, try saying, "I'm happy to be going to this party I was invited to" and see how that feels.

Someone told me once that if something is a "maybe" then it's really a "no." How true is that? We know without a doubt when something is a yes. Of course, sometimes we do things we may not be excited about because it's important to someone we love, but at the same time, it's important we have enough room in our life to honor our own needs and wants as well. Always follow your feelings and get clear on why you are doing something. If it's for the right reasons, like "It's for someone I love" or "It makes me happy," you'll know and feel good about it.

Another way to determine truth in your body is using applied kinesiology techniques. I won't go into great depth on this, but applied kinesiology uses muscle testing to get yes or no answers from the subconscious mind. Essentially, what happens is when a question is asked of the subconscious, the body responds with movement. A good example of this is to think of going to a buffet and looking at all of the options and then noticing what happens when you see your favorite foods. Your body will naturally lean forward toward the food. Conversely, if you see something on that buffet you dislike, your body will sway backward away from it.

You can try asking yourself a question and noticing if while standing if your body sways forward or backward.

For example, if you are trying to decide whether something you've been invited to participate in is something you really want to do or if it's best for you, you can ask, "Is this event good for me?" and see if you sway forward (yes) or backward (no). This is your subconscious mind controlling the movement and responding with your true answer.

One of the easiest ways to access your subconscious mind is to sit quietly with your eyes closed and allow a conversation with yourself to happen. If you are good at meditating, you will be a natural at this. If you struggle with meditating, you can still easily learn how to ask for and receive the true answers to your deepest questions. It just takes a little practice and trusting the answers you receive. It's available to each and every one of us.

Try this. Find a quiet, comfortable space to sit in. Be sure there are no distractions and you feel relaxed and safe in the space. Close your eyes and take some deep, full breaths. Notice how your body relaxes as you breathe. Clear your mind. A good starting point is to ask if your subconscious is willing to help give you answers. You will get a reply in the form of a thought. Now, think of a question you'd like to ask yourself. Maybe it's something you've been struggling to make a decision about.

The subconscious mind is quite literal, so you will want to be specific in your questioning. Don't simply ask if it has the answer for you, ask to "Please provide me with advice that will help me with this problem." Then allow your mind to contemplate and give a response. You can ask additional questions as needed. I always like to say thank you at the end of an inner self connecting mediation, it helps build trust between you and your subconscious.

Another way to get answers from your subconscious mind is through journaling or free writing also called "stream of consciousness writing." You can write down the questions you have just as you would in a meditation. Then allow your mind to be open and write whatever comes up as you ask. Don't judge what flows from your pen, just let it come, and then you can go back and read it later. Often you may write things that don't make much sense, and this is a good thing, because you are truly letting your conscious thoughts take a backseat and are allowing your subconscious to release what it needs to. When we stop thinking and truly let our feelings direct, we get to the truth.

When you get to the chapter on ways to process emotions, this practice will be explained in more depth as you can use it not only to get answers to your questions, but to explore the feelings you have about them. It will also be helpful to feel your emotions from your past, your present, and to recognize your hopes and dreams for the future.

KEY FOR CHANGE

Learn to connect to your inner navigation system. Taking some time sitting quietly and asking yourself some questions is one of the easiest ways to check in with your subconscious and find your true answers.

Practice for a few minutes daily to begin getting comfortable with how your mind and body respond to your questions.

For example if there is something you feel conflicted about, close your eyes and think about the situation and ask yourself "how does this make me feel?" Wait for a thought to come and notice the physical sensations that accompany it.

The more you practice this, the easier it will be to trust the responses.

Also try writing down some true statements about yourself and say them out loud, then notice how your body feels as you say them.

Learning what truth feels like to you is a very helpful tool to get yourself in alignment with your hopes, dreams, fears, and goals.

CHAPTER 2

It's Getting Crowded in Here

The Guest House

This being human is a guest house.
Every morning a new arrival.

A joy, a depression, a meanness, some momentary
awareness comes as an unexpected visitor.
Welcome and entertain them all! Even if they are a
crowd of sorrows, who violently sweep your house
empty of its furniture, still treat each guest honorably.
He may be clearing you out for some new delight.

The dark thought, the shame, the malice, meet
them at the door laughing, and invite them in.

Be grateful for whoever comes, because each
has been sent as a guide from beyond.

~Rumi

I love this poem by Rumi and have it hanging on my office wall as a daily reminder to check in with my emotions and to do my best to turn none of them away. This probably sounds like a strange question, but do you know how to feel your feelings? More often than not, we are not really processing what we are feeling, and are more just being "in it" until we can "get past it." We can only ignore our emotions for so long until we become uncomfortable enough that something pushes us to action; until we reach a breaking point of sorts. Our discomfort can be a catalyst to make us want a change. Our emotions are far more powerful than our thoughts, and too often we have been taught to "stuff" our feelings down inside, or ignore them as if they would go away, when in reality they only grow and become more deeply ingrained within us.

If our humanness is a guest house and every feeling a visitor, how crowded must it be if none of them ever leave? What if they all started clamoring for space in the dwelling that is our physical being? What if we slam the door shut on them, but the whole while they are standing on our front porch, banging away to be let in? What might happen to our body? Would it begin to break down under the pressure? Would we become agitated and anxious with the constant assault of unexpressed feelings?

The answer to the latter two questions is yes, if we don't work with the feelings, the feelings will start working against us until we receive the message, they are there to deliver. If we are not acknowledging what we feel, we tend to compound problems by adding extra layers. Everyone has that one drawer in their house or desk where everything gets tossed. Over time, the drawer becomes a jumbled mess we throw things in to avoid dealing with them. Then one day, you try to open the drawer and realize it is stuck because an item shoved way in the back is caught on something. Maybe you added one too many things, and now the drawer just cannot open anymore. This is what happens with our subconscious mind, the place where all of our feelings are stored.

Early in life, we develop ideas about things based on our experiences. These ideas generally stay with us even if they don't make logical sense. When we are children, we don't always have the tools to acknowledge and understand our feelings, and often we take those things into adulthood, and we continue to add to them by confirming what we have previously experienced by replaying the same unprocessed emotions. The subconscious mind loves familiarity, even when what is familiar is uncomfortable.

One day something may come up that challenges what we know as familiar, and then like the drawer, we get stuck as well until we can clear those feelings or ideas that do not serve a positive purpose in our life.

By acknowledging and processing our feelings, we can help clear out that "junk drawer" in our subconscious mind, layer by layer, and reorganize it so that what is there can be accessed in a useful, new, and healthy way bringing about positive change in our life.

In my own life, I came to a turning point where I knew I had to start inviting in the feelings and stop slamming the door on them. There was a series of events that unfolded, and at some point, in the middle of them, I realized it was time to stop pretending I had it all figured out and like nothing bothered me at all. One day about ten years ago, I was sitting in the doctor's office feeling puzzled as to why the nurse who took me back to the room asked me if I'd brought anyone along I'd like to have join me to talk to the doctor. I said, "No, thank you, I'm ok." My boyfriend (now husband, Mark) was in the waiting room having driven there with me, but I didn't understand why I would need someone, so I declined. I thought this was curious in addition to the hushed whispering she and the receptionist took part in when I arrived.

I was here because after months of feeling sick daily and waking in the night every two to three days and vomiting all night, I knew something was wrong, but I didn't know what. I had a continual burning feeling in my stomach and felt exhausted all the time. I had been here the week before, and my doctor suggested we do some blood work. I had never really had any health problems, so I didn't find anything strange about them calling me to come back. I suspected they were going to tell me I had an ulcer or something, as I had been under a lot of stress after going through a difficult divorce the two years before and recently a long period of custody issues for my two sons.

That idea quickly changed when the doctor entered the room with a very serious look on his face. He went to his computer and looked at something for a moment, presumably my bloodwork results, then looked at me, took a step closer, and placed his hand on my shoulder. The troubled look on his face was alarming. He said, "Before I tell you anything else, I want you to know there are treatments for this." In that moment, my body tensed up, I felt dizzy and confused. I suddenly realized something very bad was coming. He paused briefly then said, "I think you may have leukemia." I felt like a balloon someone had just stuck a pin into, all the air rapidly drained from my lungs, and my body went cold.

It all suddenly made sense why I didn't only receive a phone call. Why they wanted to know if I needed someone to come back with me. Why I'd been so sick. Why I felt like daily tasks were so difficult. He started explaining what we needed to do next. I felt myself frantically trying to make sense of all of it. He asked me about other symptoms, and my hand went to my arm where I had a lump that had been growing for a while. He looked at it and then looked even more concerned.

It was all so surreal. How was this happening to me? I had two sons who needed me. I couldn't have cancer.

He suggested I go back to the lab and have the bloodwork redone, and we check it again in the off chance there was some mistake. In a daze, I agreed. He said if it didn't look better, I needed to see an oncologist. He said a bunch of other things that probably didn't even register with my brain at that time, and I can't remember now. I was in shock at what I had just been told.

I walked out to the waiting room where Mark sat, and I took his hand and said, "Let's go." Now he appeared alarmed. The look on my face told him I didn't have good news. We walked out into a long hall that led toward the lab where I needed to go to have my bloodwork redone. We paused in the corridor, and he said, "What is it?" I, still stunned, said, "He thinks I may have leukemia." I watched the color drain from his face as it surely had from mine.

This was on a Friday, so all weekend I waited. On Monday when the bloodwork came back and the doctor's office called, they told me it actually looked worse than before, and I needed to see an oncologist right away. I started imagining the worst, but I didn't cry, I just felt like everything inside me was wound up in a tight ball, and that at any moment, it would explode. In fact, looking back now I don't remember crying at all.

The next two weeks until my appointment went by in a blur. I kept trying to act normal around my sons and keep a smile on my face. Behind the mask of normalcy, I was imagining the worst possible outcome. I think I had just gone numb, and it was almost as if I had left my body and was watching a sad movie playing out. I didn't take any time to feel my emotions about this, mostly because once again, I didn't really know how. I thought just being "tough" through it was somehow a good thing.

It turned out, thankfully, I didn't have leukemia, but there was clearly still something very wrong. The oncologist was also a hematologist; a doctor who deals with blood disorders. He found I didn't have cancer but was instead extremely anemic; so much so that my iron levels didn't even register on the chart. I needed to have iron infusions because he said taking a supplement would have been like trying to fill the ocean with a bucket. Once we got my iron back up, the question now was why was I so anemic? I bounced from specialist to specialist until I was finally diagnosed with Celiac Disease. I couldn't process gluten, and my body was not absorbing iron and other nutrients because the gluten had damaged my intestines so badly. I remember prior to the diagnosis telling a friend I felt like my body was attacking itself. In fact, it was.

My emotions went from terrified to relieved, then confused, and many others in a short span of time. All were intense and all were essentially ignored by me. They were left standing on the porch outside, but now instead of screaming to come in, they were hovering together in a corner just waiting for a chance to start knocking again along with the others I had previously neglected.

What I learned after this experience was the body and mind are so inner connected, and when we are not effectively processing emotions, the subconscious mind finds ways to get our attention. It may present through mental or physical health issues. You might find yourself overwhelmed and anxious frequently, angry, unable to make decisions, or constantly struggling with being sick or in pain. What got me to start seeking help with emotional processing was, after this health crises, I became even more stressed and anxious, finding myself shaking, feeling paralyzed to make changes, and like I had no choice in anything. It was as if all of the energy from multiple difficult and/or traumatic situations were clamoring to get out of my body. In the case of my Celiac Disease, I was quite literally not able to digest some things that had happened in my life.

If I were to introduce you to that version of me and the me I am today, you would never think we were the same person. Back then, I was depressed and felt very stuck, overwhelmed, and without direction. I had gone most of my life as a walking contradiction. I was a highly sensitive person, but I was stuffing all of my emotions and acting like they didn't exist. I was slamming the door on the messenger again and again. When

I was around others, I would smile and act like everything was ok, but inside I was falling apart. It turns out I didn't have a clue how to actually feel my feelings. I might recognize I had a feeling, but it never went beyond that. Like when the doctor said he thought I had cancer, I knew I was shocked, I was scared, I was worried, but yet I didn't cry or scream or do anything. I just said, "Ok, what do I need to do?" Rather than feeling the emotions, I took on the task of making them, or the trigger for them, go away. While being able to handle things to move yourself forward is a great skill, if there are emotions stuck inside you, they are going to eventually come back asking for attention.

It was "normal" for me to just deal with things and think I had to be strong all the time, which I equated to "Don't cry, just get it together and figure this out." If you are reading this and thinking "I do that too," it's time to let those houseguests in, hear the story they have to tell, and let them go on their way.

When I began processing my emotions about things that had happened in my life, I began to feel better. In fact, I can't remember the last time I had a Celiac symptom. Yes, I am careful to not eat gluten, but previously I was still getting sick almost every time I ate in a restaurant or ate something I didn't prepare myself. This no longer happens. While I won't say emotional processing "cured" me, I can't dispute finally addressing emotions that had been long trapped in my body has made an extremely positive impact on my improved health. In addition to better physical health, I found my anxiety went away, and I became clearer about what I wanted in life and who I was. By finally opening the door to my feelings, I was able to make huge changes in my life.

We have negative emotions because things have happened in our life to make us feel that way. Our feelings are valid, they are important, and they need to be heard and respected. If we allow ourselves to actually feel our emotions, our lives improve, our joy increases, and our overall well-being is enhanced. This is why our feelings truly matter. We need to be present with our emotions, so we can be present in our world, not bogged down with anger, sadness, grief, resentment, and despair.

Sometimes healing is like having a messy closet. I don't know about you, but I used to struggle with keeping my closet neat. I'd hang onto things long past when I should have. Even if I wasn't wearing them anymore, I couldn't bear to part with them. I'd leave them hanging there, "just in case" I needed that particular kind of dress again or if I might get something to go with those shoes, I had to have but never wore. I'd just keep adding to the mess, bringing in new shirts, jeans, and handbags. Very infrequently would I really clean things out. Once I thought I'd categorize everything into types of clothes, like tee shirts in one section, long sleeves in another, then I arranged them by color too. This didn't last long. It felt awesome to see it that way, but the reality was I couldn't sustain it because I just had way too many items I didn't wear cluttering things up.

In our messy closet, we can walk in, and all these things are kind of falling on us, and we don't know what to do with them. There may be unfolded sweaters, shoes in piles, blouses recklessly hanging off hangers, and a clothes basket with clothes from the dryer yet to be put in their correct place. Likewise, our feelings can be in our "emotional closet" in the form of tears stuffed down from a loss we never got through, anger brimming over after a long-ago argument, or hot shame from something we wish we had not done. We know there's a problem, but trying to figure out how to organize the mess feels overwhelming.

So instead of doing anything about it, we push the door shut tightly and hope it doesn't bust out into our other living spaces. Unfortunately, the door usually cracks open, and much like when unannounced guests arrive and we haven't tidied up, our feelings can spill out at inopportune times, creating a bigger mess and only contributing to more disarray in our lives. Sometimes we just need someone to help us see a better way to organize, to know what to purge, what to consolidate, and what to replace with something new, like a new thought, or a new belief that better matches our goals and dreams.

That person may be a professional closet organizer (if we are still talking about your wardrobe!) or a therapist trained in helping people walk through past traumas, or sometimes it's a friend we can confide in who may just hold space for us as we work our way through the darkness. This assistance can also come in the form of a class, a book, or a method of healing you do on your own. There are many roads to the same destination, and sometimes we have to make a few U-turns in the process. The roads you take aren't the important part, what's important is you begin the trip.

I recently visited an amusement park with my two now adult sons. The park was two-and-a-half hours from our house. There were several route options given by my GPS, and as crazy as it sounds, I took the longest one. I took it because it was more scenic with options of places to stop if needed. I also preferred the back roads to the main highways. It took us a little longer to get there, but we were more relaxed on the trip. What I'm trying to say is this whole "healing" process doesn't need to go at warp speed. Take your time, know there is a lot happening along the way, and you don't need to be overly stressed to reap the benefits by trying to get there right now. Remember, we are all works in progress, and that progress will continue to happen for your entire life, so by all means, enjoy the journey!

One morning I took a walk in the rain. It started out as light rain but was soon pouring. Even though it was mid-June, it was very cool, and by the time I returned four miles later, I was shivering. I went directly to the shower and turned the water to hot, put my hand under the spray, and immediately pulled it back because it felt like it was scalding. I looked at the handle and where it was turned to, and logic told me the water was not as hot as it felt to my numb hand. I kept pulling it back out and turning the temperature down. Eventually I stepped into the shower and let my body acclimate. In no time, the water felt cold, and I turned it up a bit. As I did, I began thinking about how this experience was like feeling one's feelings.

Sometimes we become numb to what we feel, and then when we try to start feeling, things get really intense. We might be overwhelmed with emotion in the process. The good news is, much like how my body adjusted to the temperature, those intense feelings don't last too long, and soon we are relieved of the uncomfortable sensations. Don't be afraid to turn up the dial and let your emotions be known, when you do, your body and mind will thank you.

KEY FOR CHANGE

Our feelings are like visitors, they come for a while, but do not have to stay. We have the option and the power to determine how long they are with us, but we must first open the door so they can come in or they will just keep knocking.

If we ignore our feelings, they will eventually find a way to get our attention. This may come in the form of anxiety, overwhelm, or consistent stress. Sometimes the emotions will also make their appearance via physical symptoms.

Take some time thinking about if you find yourself repeatedly experiencing strong negative feelings or physical pain. Create a space in your journal to document your emotions. You can note the day, frequency, and trigger for something and see if there are patterns in how often and under what circumstances something is coming up for you. This will give you clues to understanding what is happening in your subconscious and will be helpful as you begin to work through those feelings.

Jetsam and Flotsam

The only place that a feeling will hurt you is when it is left inside you. Yes, something can be painful at the time it occurs, but if we acknowledge it in the moment, we will have better results than when we avoid feeling it. We have to allow ourselves to feel even the hardest, most painful things so that they don't accumulate and multiply. If we don't feel our feelings, the repercussions of holding them in will eventually catch up to us. For a while it might seem ok, you might tell yourself "I've got this," but as time goes on, you will likely feel the pressure and overwhelm rise. You might find it's hard to keep all of your emotions from spilling out randomly. Take a moment and notice patterns in your life. They might be in relationships, or career, or how you feel about yourself, but any place a negative pattern is playing out again and again, you are dealing with an unhealed emotion that needs to be heard and felt.

While working on this book, I had a dream that was really just a set of words. I woke up, and those words kept repeating in my mind. The really interesting thing was I couldn't place what the words meant. I knew I'd heard them before, but they were not part of my daily vocabulary, so it was puzzling I dreamed them. They kept coming back to me over the course of two days until finally I looked them up. The words were "jetsam and flotsam." After an online dictionary search, I found they are nautical terms. I still didn't know why I woke with these words in my head, I wasn't dreaming of boats, but the more I read, the more it made sense.

Flotsam is defined as debris in the water that was not deliberately thrown overboard from a ship, typically from a shipwreck or accident. While jetsam is debris that has been thrown overboard intentionally, typically by a ship in distress trying to lighten its load to avoid wrecking. After I read these definitions, I had an aha moment as to why I dreamed this.

I often receive guidance through my dreams. I will sometimes dream words or songs that have messages to be conveyed to me. In this case as I had been working on this book, things were coming as topics to write about. I have no other explanation for this as I didn't know what the words even meant, but when I finally looked them up, they stopped playing on repeat in my mind.

Our feelings can be like jetsam and flotsam too. There are the feelings we don't intentionally let spill out, but they often do anyway. Our flotsam can come in the form of angry outbursts at undeserving people, or bossiness because of a need to control, or maybe our anxious feelings hold us back from doing things. Conversely, we can take those same feelings and instead make them jetsam by processing with intention, and instead of carelessly throwing them onto others, we are able to integrate what we learn from really feeling them and lighten our own load, so we don't wreck, so to speak.

Recently, my mom had a surgery and in her month-long recovery, she was very limited on what she was allowed to do. This seemed like an incredible challenge to my mom, who is a mover and a shaker, and sitting still and not lifting and not doing much was definitely not her way of being. One day she texted me that for the last two days, she had been working on cleaning out her email. She had over 12,000 emails, and over the course of two days, got it down to 300. I think her inability to do much for that time made it very satisfying to watch the number drop in her inbox. How wonderful would it be to take all the junk we've held onto for so long and start clearing it out emotionally too? How much lighter might you feel? How much clearer might things be?

Things get muddy when we have all kinds of feelings moving around us. Imagine a storm with branches, leaves, dirt, and other debris flying around in a cloud. You can't see the clear sky ahead because of all the chaos. This is how emotions work too. If we are in the middle of a storm of feelings, we can't see that it's temporary. Our vision is clouded, our perception is it will always be this bad. However, if we begin to take those emotions one at a time and explore where they are coming from and work through them, we can find relief and make decisions based on clear thought. The wind stops howling, the rain stops pouring, and we start to see the blue sky ahead. It doesn't mean it never rains again, but instead, you'll have longer periods of time with calmness and clarity surrounding you.

You can avoid the stuck point in many instances by learning to recognize when the storm is picking up and start working with those feelings as they arise. By checking in with ourselves and honoring whatever feeling comes up, we are helping ourselves avoid a lot of unnecessary suffering in the future. On the other side of strong emotion is always a clarity point.

Have you ever walked past something that smells really bad, like a garbage truck, or a field that has just been fertilized? The odor might assault your nose and burn your throat. It might even make you feel a little sick. You can try to hold your breath, to avoid breathing it in, to keep yourself from having to smell it, but as you're holding your breath if it takes a while to get past it, you might start to feel uncomfortable, you might feel like there's no air in your lungs anymore. Sometimes that's how we deal with things in life that are really uncomfortable, and instead of trying to get through it, we try to hurry around it, or avoid the area altogether and maybe pretend we don't feel what we feel. The problem is that garbage truck eventually comes around your block again on the next garbage day, or they fertilize the field again, or the walk you take still goes past a smelly barn. When we ignore our feelings, we might feel better for a moment like covering our mouth and nose or by telling ourselves it doesn't bother us, but eventually that feeling bubbles up again, and it will continue to do so over and over until we finally face it

So why does it matter if I feel my feelings? Oftentimes we get to a "stuck" point in our lives. We may think we just don't know what to do about a situation or see a way to change our mindset about something. We may begin to accept this is "just the way it is for me." There's good news though, we do not have to accept less than we want in our lives. The easiest way out of the stuck point is to process our emotions. It is always the answer. We must first change our feelings so we can change our thoughts.

 ## KEY FOR CHANGE

Points to remember:

The only place a feeling can hurt you is when you leave it stuck inside. Yes, it may hurt as you process it, but that is temporary. Ignoring your negative emotions is painful for the long term.

When we don't acknowledge our feelings, it's more likely we will let them spill out in ways we don't want them to and find ourselves triggered over and over again, creating more pain in our lives.

We can choose with intention to process our emotions rather than letting our emotions be the ones in control.

All Feelings Are Good

Although the world is full of suffering, it is also full of the overcoming it. ~Helen Keller, Optimism

I'm sure you've heard this statement before, but the only way out is through. The alternative rock band O.A.R. has a song called "I Go Through." The main refrain of the song says, "you go round and around it, you go over and under, I go through." Every time I hear this song, I think about how if we dance around something we need to heal, we will never truly get through it. Nothing will change. We can't go over and under something forever. Eventually, we must go through it, we must pull apart every ugly detail, every painful issue, and feel the feelings, to find clarity about it if we hope to live our lives authentically.

When working with someone, I assure them all feelings are good. That statement surely sounds confusing though, because all feelings may not make us happy or feel good, but all feelings are present to convey information to us, and therefore are good in that regard. Think of them as messengers. The positive feelings we have tell us when we are on the right track, when we are doing what makes us happy, and creates authenticity in our lives. The negative feelings let us know when something needs to change, when we are not being true to ourselves, and what is best for us. Without our feelings to guide us, it's like going on a trip without a GPS or a map. I don't know about you, but I wouldn't get very far without some navigational tools. This is the same for life. Our feelings are like our co-pilot, guiding us and telling us when and where to turn, when to stop, when to go, or when to change direction all together.

In addition to all feelings being good as messengers, all feelings we have are valid as well. Every last one of them. Please don't ever tell yourself, or anyone else for that matter, what you or they should or shouldn't feel. Before I had my first son, I had been pregnant another time and miscarried in the fourteenth week. When I found out the baby had died in my womb, it was one of a handful of experiences in my life where I felt time had literally stopped, and I was outside watching rather than participating. I didn't know it then, but years later, I understood it was so painful, I had completely checked out emotionally as a way to cope with the overwhelming realization I was losing my baby. I remember the day like it was yesterday, although, it's now almost twenty-five years later. I went to a routine doctor appointment, and when the midwife placed the doppler on my abdomen to find the baby's heartbeat, she couldn't seem to locate it. I remember feeling a little alarmed, but she calmed me by saying we would try an ultrasound because maybe the baby was positioned funny and was preventing her from finding it. After moving to a low-lit area with a curtain pulled around it and laying back on the bed, I could see the baby on the screen, but by the look on the midwife's face, I knew something wasn't right. She quietly said, "I'm going to go get the doctor." As she left, I looked at my husband, feeling panicked, and I said, "It's not ok, is it?" He just shook his head looking somber.

The doctor came in and confirmed my worst fear. He said, "The baby doesn't have a heartbeat, I'm so sorry." I had so many feelings in that moment, but I didn't have the ability to do anything with them. It felt like it wasn't real, this wasn't really happening to me. It felt like I would wake up and realize it was just a nightmare. But it wasn't. It was true, painfully, agonizingly true.

It was surprising to me how they did almost nothing to help me through it. They told me to go have my blood drawn, so they could monitor the levels of human growth hormones in my body. They said as the hormone levels dropped; I would eventually spontaneously miscarry. If a week passed and nothing happened, then they would intervene. I remember walking to the counter to get my blood drawn and feeling like I wasn't really even there.

I was wearing a long-sleeved white shirt and a red jacket. It was a chilly early spring day, and as I went back to the car, I felt like my arm where they had drawn the blood was so extremely cold. I pulled it out of my jacket and saw the shirt I was wearing was no longer white, but my entire sleeve was soaked in blood. This added to the trauma for me. It was like an outward sign of what was to come.

I was completely devastated, and in shock. I walked around in a daze waiting for the inevitable physical loss of my dreamed of baby. It took five days of waiting for my body to naturally miscarry, and every moment felt like torture. I cried constantly, but even though I was crying, I wasn't really doing anything with the emotion. I was sitting in it with no way out. It was like it was drowning me. My emotional pain began to consume me. I wanted nothing more than to have a baby, and now I didn't even know if it was possible. To make matters worse, there seemed to be a baby boom among my friends, and I kept receiving joyful news from friend after friend about their new pregnancies. I remember standing in the shower feeling like my heart was being completely crushed. I was blaming myself, going over every supplement I had taken, every workout I had done, every food I'd eaten. Surely, I must have caused this.

I was trying so hard to be happy for my friends, and while I was happy for them, I couldn't ignore the fact I was so very sad for myself. Someone close to me told me I needed to just be happy for everyone else, and my time would come. I wanted to believe that, but would it really? I didn't find this statement helpful. What I really needed was someone to come to me and say, please, feel your sorrow, grieve your loss, you are allowed to feel this. I ended up pushing those feelings down for a long, long time. I was ignoring what I was feeling, and again even though I was crying often, I wasn't doing anything to actually move the emotion or integrate it into anything helpful. Yes, I did eventually go on to have two healthy, wonderful sons, but I also ached for the baby I never held, and that sorrow would still come up sometimes over a period of many years.

Thankfully, I eventually learned how to process my feelings and access my subconscious mind to find healing about the situation. I still hold my lost baby in my heart, but now I know what happened wasn't my fault, and there was likely something wrong with the baby, and he probably wouldn't have survived if I had carried him to term. I finally allowed myself to feel the grief, the sorrow, and the anguish I had stuffed away for so long, and that was a tremendous gift to myself. I now think of my third son as an angel watching over me, and that makes me smile.

If I had not learned how to walk through the fire of loss and allow all of the feelings to come up and be heard, I might never have found peace or acceptance of what happened, and certainly not forgiveness for myself. I had to stop going around and around it, I had to go through it, and really feel it, so I could step out of the emotion and truly move forward.

I shared this story because I want you to understand even when we think we have moved past something emotionally traumatic, so often we have in fact just found some way to move around it, and we have not truly gone through it. We may feel like we are not affected by it, but the truth is, something may trigger it because the original emotions were never fully addressed.

I am a distance runner, and while it is physically good for me, I also get a lot of emotional benefit and inspiration from the process. One morning doing a hill workout which involved running up and down a hill over and over again (sounds fun, right?), I realized something about that was similar to the healing process. The particular workout I was doing had me sprinting up the hill as far as I could go for thirty seconds. When the timer went off, I would walk back down and then do it again. I repeated this process six times. Each time I tried to get just a few steps further. It was hard, but the interesting thing was even with how difficult it was, I noticed I was in fact getting a bit higher on the hill each time. Even as I got tired, my body had adjusted to the effort, and I was able to give a little more and get another step or two.

How is this like healing? Well, I think when we are persistent with recognizing and working through our feelings, it gets easier. Yes, it's still hard, but we adjust and push on. The payoff with the hill repeats is when I get to my race, my body feels more prepared and capable of getting through the difficult parts. With emotional processing, it's the same thing. We know there's something really good on the other side of the pain. Something may hurt for the moment, but it doesn't last, and in fact, it feels like a great relief when we clearly can see and understand what the pain was about in the first place.

I had a client who had literally experienced a lifetime of trauma. She had been through one painful experience after another. However, she came to me with a sunshine in her soul. She didn't let the difficulties completely drag her down, which quite honestly would have been easy to do. Instead, she looked at where she had been, where she was, and ultimately where she wanted to go. She took those points and decided facing the hard stuff head on was the only way to move through it.

Within about a half dozen sessions, she felt completely different about her past. She was able to find the lessons and blessings within them and that light she held within burned brighter. She had taken the painful emotions and the stories behind them and let them be way markers rather than anchors. This can be the truth for anyone. All you need is a desire for something different, and a willingness to truly experience the pain, so that it can reveal the greater gifts within.

KEY FOR CHANGE

Points to remember:

All feelings are good. All feelings may not make us feel good or happy, but they are good in the sense they provide us with valuable information about where we are and where we want to go.

All feelings are valid. Do not allow another person to tell you your feelings are not valid, and likewise, do not tell yourself that either. The truth is if you are feeling something, something in your life has happened to create that feeling. Acknowledge, respect, and feel your feelings. You deserve that.

We must go through our painful experiences to find the lessons and blessings they offer. We cannot go over, under, or around them and get those results. Through is the only way.

Shake it Off

There are many different ways and therapies to process your emotions, but the subconscious mind will always be involved as it is the storage place for your feelings. Our unprocessed emotions can be the culprit of many difficulties in life, and working through them is the solution.

Accessing the subconscious mind is tremendously helpful to not only work through major traumas and events, but also for the day to day finding of answers to questions we have about the direction we are headed in life. What it comes down to is having a conversation with your subconscious, and sometimes that is talking to a feeling or to a younger version of you, whether it is decades younger or weeks younger. It's learning how to trust the messages you receive and to allow yourself to really experience your truest emotions.

Following the same process, I described in the chapter on accessing your subconscious mind, you'll find a quiet place without distractions. You'll want the place you choose to sit to be comfortable and make you feel at ease. The less focused on outside influences you are, the better. Once you find this place, simply close your eyes. Next, take some deep and complete breaths. Try not to think about anything other than how it feels to fill your lungs with air and exhale fully. Continue breathing in this manner until you truly feel like you have released tension and expectation.

When your mind is clear, ask this question (you can state the question out loud or simply think it), "Is there any version of me who needs to be heard today?" And then just wait while continuing to breathe and focus on the question.

You might see in your mind yourself at a younger age, or you might suddenly remember an event from your past. Trust there are answers to be found within these thoughts. If you see yourself at a younger age, imagine you are sitting down next to that earlier you. Now, have a conversation with that you. Think of it as if you were talking with a trusted friend.

This part might seem a little tricky at first, but I promise with practice it will get easier. Here's a very important key to remember. You will receive your answers as thoughts. Because you are the one asking the question *and* answering it, it will all come via your own thoughts. Everyone is a little different in this depending on how your brain works. Some people will just seem to know what the reply is, while others will "see" an image in their mind. While still others will "hear" the words as if a person has spoken to them. The method of delivery isn't so important as just knowing however the answer is given, it is coming from your subconscious mind.

You can also try speaking to an emotion you are experiencing. For example, you might be feeling angry sensations. You might even think you know why you feel that way. Something may have happened that day to upset you, and you might be feeling quite angry. However, there may be more to it than that. There may be a message in that anger about a previous situation, or about the current situation that has more answers for you within. Because the subconscious is the keeper of your feelings, asking questions about it will help you find clarity about the emotion, and also about what you may need to do to feel better or move forward from it.

So, here's what you can do. With your eyes still closed, you will want to think of that emotion and visualize yourself sitting down with the feeling and then asking the feeling what message it has for you. You could phrase the question this way: "Anger, what is it that you are trying to tell me? What do I need to know about you?" Allow the answer to come. Perhaps it will be a reminder of a previous time when you were angry and that coming up now may be a clue you need to go back and work through that time in the past when something made you angry. Oftentimes, if we haven't resolved an old emotion, it will get triggered anytime we have the same emotion even if the situation that is creating it is completely different.

Here are some more examples of connecting to the subconscious mind, and these are without conscious intention to do so, but they still helped the people in the examples at least begin to recognize feelings they were having. We are always looking for opportunities to make sense of our life experiences whether we realize it or not. In these examples, you'll see how some everyday things can really be a stepping-stone to creating order and expression of our emotions.

I was working with someone once who was telling me about a car accident they had had in the past. This person was a very math minded individual, and they told me that after the accident, they set up some mathematical equations about how much force was inflicted on their body in the impact of the accident. As they were describing the distance the car that hit them came from and how fast they were going among other things, it occurred to me it certainly wasn't fun to make up a math problem about something that was traumatic, so there had to be another reason they had done this. As we continued to talk, I realized what they had accomplished in this exercise. They didn't realize what they were doing was giving validation to the fact they were allowed to have felt pain, shock, and fear. For them, they needed something concrete, something they could see on paper in order to feel something.

I said, "Do you know you are processing the accident with your numbers?" It was in that moment I saw that because we all have brains that work in different ways, we all will find different ways to work through our emotions. For me, doing a math problem would probably create more trauma, but for them, it brought them peace and validation.

Connecting with things that make us feel nostalgic can also be healing. Have you ever seen something from your childhood and suddenly felt a flood of memories coming back? In doing so, your subconscious is recalling happy times, and that can foster a positive outlook especially if things have been difficult recently. We are reminded of times when we felt safe, loved, and happy. On a trip home recently, I had the opportunity to drive through the area I grew up in which was about twenty-five minutes away from where my mom and stepdad live now.

When I graduated, they moved from my childhood home, and so the times I went back to the neighborhood my younger self had lived in had been infrequent. I was taken aback by how small everything felt and appeared to me. As a child, the streets felt so long when I was racing to the bus stop hoping to make it before hearing the door close and the heavy bus pull away. Now it felt like they were so short. The houses looked almost "squished" to me, seeming so much smaller than I remembered.

Driving past the little post office to which it was my job to walk to after descending the bus, with the mailbox key clutched tightly in my hand, evoked a smell in my memory that was so distinct, a mixture of paper, cardboard, and ink.

I drove through the little town up one street and down an-other, trying to recall who lived where and what it felt like to ride my bike down a hill that seemed so much steeper all those years ago. I was trying to decide whether it really was that much smaller, or if I was just much bigger now. That may be a matter of perspective…as with anything. I think we see what we need and want to see, not necessarily how some-thing is. It was not lost on me I was no longer the little girl who so quietly tried to blend in with her surroundings, shy and unsure. Maybe I was seeing the town so much smaller not because I was physically bigger, but because I had grown in other ways too since I had lived there.

Someone I know started a collection recreating items from their childhood; a childhood that was not particularly happy. They had been raised in a very dysfunctional and abusive home, and fear was something instilled in them daily. They, however, cherished their treasured toys, books, and music. As they were working on their collection, I asked if there was something healing about it. They said they needed to think about it and would get back to me. A few days later, they reported they had figured out what was helpful and healing in recreating the happy things from those years. They told me even though their home life was scary and uncomfort-able, they had a little world of their own with their few prized possessions. As an adult, they had been on a healing jour-ney and were learning about how the past had shaped their present. They recognized in gathering these items again, they were reminded while there was a lot of negativities in their upbringing, there were in fact some good things. It served as a powerful reminder that even in the midst of difficulty and pain, they had some positive things to anchor them in the present moment. It was helpful to them now to begin to shift from the fearful and negative feelings that would come up any time something was out of the status quo for them. The collection served as a talisman of sorts, a touchstone to staying in the moment and recognizing the good around them.

Healing can come in surprising ways too. We never know exactly when a moment of healing will arrive. Many years ago, I was working for a government agency in Washington, DC, when 9/11 happened. We had a number of our employees who lost their lives in the Pentagon that day, and our agency wanted to create a memorial to honor those lives lost. I was working in the multimedia department and was assigned to work on this project. We had several components to the memorial we designed that needed to be outsourced and built. One of them entailed having a mold of a metal book. I worked with many different vendors working out the details of this project, and the owner of the foundry that created the metal book later sent me a beautiful letter thanking me for allowing him to work on this project. He had been struggling with some things related to the Vietnam War which he had fought in as a young man. He told me working on this project was tremendously healing for him, it was a way for him to recall feelings he'd had about things he had experienced and lives that were lost around him. Sometimes a healing moment comes along without us even considering we needed it. Perhaps when we have pushed the feelings away for so long, we almost convince ourselves they are gone, even though they are not.

I've also noticed some people find healing in learning more about their family background. Delving into family trees, searching out lineages, names, characteristics, and skills of ancestors. It's almost as if what they see in family who is in front of them doesn't make sense, so they go digging in the past to try and understand who they are and where they came from. I know multiple people who have experienced trauma in their lives and have done extensive family history searching and documenting. I asked one of them why they feel so drawn to it, and I was told one of the reasons was they felt connected to loved ones they had been close to, but also it helped them see traits they have that they didn't quite understand where they had come from. In one case, a person found their family was not technically related by blood, but they still felt honored to have that person's name because they had done something very upstanding in taking in a young pregnant woman who later was to become the great-grandmother to that person. It seems to help to find people in one's family history who align with them perhaps better than living and or known family members.

For someone else, emotional processing may come out in journaling, or singing, or painting. Some of us may have a combination of ways to move through our feelings, and that can be very helpful too. In that case, it's like if you try one door and it is locked, you can always try another. We may not get to the core of a really deep issue through working on an art project, but we may become aware of what it is we need to look at, or start to take off the first layer of feelings. Awareness creates momentum to change.

Movement is a great way to get emotions flowing. When we move our body physically, we also move our emotions. Walking, running, jumping on a trampoline, shaking your arms and legs, taking an aerobics class, dancing, or riding a bike can help open the pathways to access your subconscious mind, and let those feelings come to the surface. Have you seen how a dog shakes after being in an altercation with another dog, or after being in a stressful situation, meeting someone new or experiencing something scary? It's as if they want to shake off the intensity of the moment. Dogs literally "shake off" what is stressful to them. It's a reset so they don't carry that stress energy with them. We can take a lesson from our pets and learn to shake off some of the emotional charge from a situation.

These activities alone may not completely process a feeling, but anything that begins to make us look inside is going to help. We can't enter a room if we haven't opened the door. We have to get curious about what we are feeling and look for ways to begin to work through it in order to make changes.

Have you ever noticed how much better you feel after you have a good cry? I'm talking about crying for a good bit of time, really letting out the stress, sadness, overwhelm, anger, or whatever else comes up. The next time you cry, pay attention afterward to how much better you feel through this act alone. There is a reason for this. The body releases endorphins through the act of crying. The oxytocin released helps with both physical and emotional pain and creates a new, calm feeling within the body. So, if you feel like you need to cry, do it, you'll be better for it.

A tool I use with hypnotherapy clients is Emotional Freedom Technique or EFT. It involves tapping on points on the hands, face, and body as a method of emotional releasing that is widely used in all types of therapy, and when used correctly, it can have a huge impact on transforming negative emotions and bringing clarity to situations. This technique can be used in conjunction with other therapies as I use it, or it is also extremely effective on its own.

The EFT practice starts with acknowledging a feeling you have, and then declaring that it's ok to feel that way. There is a huge impact to the subconscious mind by simply saying you are allowed to feel something. We so often deny our feelings. But think about it, if are walking around in pain or confusion, how much power there is in validating that for yourself.

Try this. Think of how you are feeling about something right now, and then say that you do feel that way. For example: **I *do* feel angry, I *do* feel hurt, I *do* feel lost, I *do* feel confused,** etc. How much relief do you get from the statement alone? Pause and consider. Try repeating the statement. Notice what the words feel like. Notice what your body feels like.

Then you want to declare even though you feel whatever the emotion is, you completely accept yourself. Like this: I do feel angry, and even though I feel angry, I accept myself.

You are giving yourself permission to feel the truth of your emotions, and you are accepting that it is ok to feel whatever it is. It's also important to declare you do not want to hang onto your negative feeling, by saying you want to release it. You might say something like this: "I feel angry. Even though I feel angry, I accept myself. I do not want to hang onto this anger, I want to let it pass through my body, so I can feel better." You would then continue to state the feeling you have while tapping on the acupressure points that are used with this method of emotional releasing. As you follow the process, you will receive information from your subconscious mind about the feeling, and in most cases, you will find clarity to help you move forward. You can get a lot of emotional relief following this process. It's a great stress relieving tool as well. To learn more about EFT/Tapping go to my website: Jennifer-Riggs. com for videos and downloadable resources.

Acknowledge your feelings and allow yourself to move through them.

It's ok to feel whatever you feel. It's not wrong to feel something. So often people will be hesitant to say they hate someone, but the truth is, you might really feel that. More often than not, it's the actions of the person you hate, but it feels like you hate them because the actions are so painful. If you take time to work through your feelings about the actions, you will be able to get a clear picture of how you really feel about them and if there is more to be worked through with this person. The reality is negative emotions trapped in your body about another person do not hurt them, they hurt you. So, while it may feel like you hate them, if you take time to work through the emotion, you will most likely see it was really how they hurt you that you hate, not the person. By acknowledging the emotion, you will not only be able to release the emotion but also free yourself from that emotional stronghold. You have the power to change your feelings, but it has to start with actually feeling them and giving them a voice.

These are just some ways to begin to process your emotions. Talking with a trusted therapist if you need help in getting to the core of something is also a good idea, and if you don't know where to begin, that might be the best idea. The first step to making changes and working through emotions is recognizing that you need and want to do it.

KEY FOR CHANGE

Are you ready to take active steps to begin to acknowledge and really feel your feelings so that you can find relief and clarity?

There are many different ways to process emotions and what works for one person may not work for another, so be open to trying different things until you find what fits best for you.

Commit to starting a practice of acknowledging and processing your emotions today and get ready for positive things to happen in your life. You don't have to do it all at once, but the only way to make change is to begin.

Visit my website **Jennifer-Riggs.com** for more guidance on emotional processing.

CHAPTER 3

Positivity Doesn't Come First

Sometimes Positivity is Just Denial

~ Whitney Goodman, *Toxic Positivity*

What about just being positive?

Oh, if only it were that simple!

Have you ever noticed on social media people who one day will post something all about thinking positive and about having "good vibes only," and then the next day they will make three posts about everything wrong in their life? They will then follow up with a couple positive posting days and jump back into all of the problems a few days later.

Hear me out, this is not a judgment of them, there is a reason why they are doing this. If this is you, know I see you, and I used to do this too (I see the evidence of it when my Facebook memories come up). I think there is value in sharing positive posts and in staying positive; however, if we are only saying it, and not actually doing it, not truly *feeling* it, we just stay in a cycle of repeating the same behaviors and we never really change anything. We aren't becoming more positive, we are just repeating familiar behaviors, trying to express what we want, but not acknowledging where we actually are.

The reason people can't maintain the positive posts or positive thinking is because they are trying to convince themselves everything is great and wonderful in their life, but subconsciously, they are hurting and maybe not really even realizing it. Of course, no one is going to have all positive days, no matter how much healing work they've done. However, you don't have to stay stuck in an endless cycle trying to pretend things are ok when they are not. So, when you have a bad day, you might opt to not post anything rather than share something that tells a story of you as a victim. Does that mean we can't ever share our bad days or difficulties? No, of course not, but there's a difference between sharing to find support and sharing because it somehow makes us feel good when things aren't going well for us. Believe it or not, some people really do find comfort in that, but it's only because it's a story they are telling themselves about who they are and it's familiar and known to them. I've seen people post about really bad days they have had, but they have followed up with what that event taught them. It has a different feel than angry, negative posting.

Have you ever painted a room in your house? If you have, you know before you begin, you need to look at the wall and see if there are any marks on the surface or any holes that need patching. You'd then clean and prep the wall, and typically, you would apply a primer next before brushing on your fresh new color. This is the order for being able to absorb positive mantras too. If we want real change to take place, we've got to really feel into what's locking us down. Otherwise, we are merely painting over a dirty surface, and eventually, the dark stuff shows through.

When I was working with clients one-on-one in my office, I would point to an area rug and say, "If I sweep dirt under this rug every day, is the dirt ever really gone just because we can't see it anymore?" Of course, the answer was no. So, if I keep sweeping the dirt under the rug, I might not see it on first glance, but if I look a little closer, I might see where the rug bulges a bit, where it's piled up. The only way for the dirt to be truly gone is to sweep it up and remove it. The same goes for our negative feelings. In order to be able to have the positive mindset that really stays with us, we must take out the hurtful things and work through them to some resolution so that we can feel better and make room for the new, better way of thinking.

Having positive mantras is great for compounding what you are working on. So, if you are working on self-image, you might say, "My body is beautiful just as it is." This might not feel true for you at first, but continuing to say it daily in addition to working through the emotions of why you have poor body image is a great pairing to really solidify your new beliefs.

People who think positively and maintain it are typically able to do so because they not only have walked through their story, but they have chosen to own it, the good and the bad. They are able to see the growth points they've had, and the ways difficult things have indeed had a positive impact on them for the long term. Of course, it's far better to say positive mantras to yourself even if you haven't processed your painful emotions than it is to be negative all the time, but to have real change, we must do both.

Weighing the two options of thinking negatively and thinking positively, which one is more appealing to you? Let's look at the negative thoughts first. If you are thinking negatively, you are likely telling yourself a story about who you are that isn't true. You are imagining the worst in situations, believing things cannot change, and life is just plain hard no matter what you do. Remember, you are only thinking that way because you have not felt your true feelings and processed them so that you can make room for what it is you really want. A positive life is available to you when you choose to feel and move through your negative experiences and create a place for the positive mindset to thrive.

KEY FOR CHANGE:

In order to have a positive mindset, we must first address our negative emotions. We can't just try to cover negative feelings with positive ones. We must create space for new, better ways of thinking.

Positive mantras are helpful and will compound our new positive mindset after we have processed our feelings. What is a positive mantra you can start using today to compound a change you would like to make in your life? Write it down and put it someplace you will see it and say it often.

CHAPTER 4

JOINED AT THE HIP

The mind and body are not separate,
what affects one affects the other.

~ Unknown

Our body and mind are inextricably connected, as I mentioned I learned when describing the health situation, I experienced all those years ago. The body remembers because the mind does and vice versa. Have you ever injured yourself, but then long after the injury has healed, you find yourself protecting that area? Your mind remembers the trauma of the injury, and even though the pain is gone, there may be a desire to protect yourself. If so, there's likely some emotion attached to the injury that triggers the desire to create a shield. Now, think about how that might apply to other situations. If you've been hurt in a relationship, the emotions you may have pushed down or stuffed away can be keeping you from feeling safe in venturing into a new relationship with your whole heart. The desire to protect your heart can be as literal as the desire to protect yourself where a previous physical injury was incurred.

When we ignore what we feel, we can create a whole host of problems ranging from depression, anxiety, pain, disease, and a variety of physical ailments. If you start having physical pain, take a moment with your eyes closed to ask yourself, is there a feeling I am ignoring? The body and mind are one and the same. The lines begin to blur, and if you are not responding to emotional pain, the body may use physical pain to get your attention. If you have children or have been around children, you know what it's like when a child is tugging on your pants leg asking to be heard. This is a visual for what the subconscious mind does to get an opportunity to work through emotional things. Maybe you start getting headaches, or a nagging pain in your shoulder or back, maybe you keep having an upset stomach or a recurring infection. Of course, if you believe there is something going on with your health, it's best to see a doctor. However, you can also begin working with your subconscious to find out what you might need to be listening to from your inner voice.

One way to access this valuable information in your subconscious is to use the method I explained of sitting quietly with your eyes closed, and in the case of working through physical pain that might be coming from emotions, let your attention go to the part of you that is hurting. So, if your back hurts, begin thinking of your back. You can even talk to your back and say something like "Do you have a message for me in this pain?" Allow whatever message that comes to your mind be there. It's always best to trust the subconscious, and even if something comes to mind you think couldn't possibly be the issue, give it the opportunity to be heard. If something comes to conscious awareness, there is generally a reason.

We can have physical reactions to emotions and not even realize it. During one marathon training cycle, my running partner got injured just before we had a twenty-mile run on our schedule. I didn't want to run alone, so when I was invited by a group of women who were a good bit faster than me to come run with them, I was anxious to say the least. The day of the run, I held my own and for the most part didn't need them to slow down too much for me. I was pretty pleased with this, but on the ten-minute drive home, my legs began to cramp up in a way I had not experienced before. By the time I got home, I could barely get out of the car it hurt so much. The cramping continued while I showered and dressed, and then it occurred to me I might have some emotions needing to be processed.

My body was giving me a message through the pain. I knew I needed to process whatever it was in order to feel better, so I closed my eyes and immediately it came to mind I felt a lack of control about the run. I could feel how stressed I had been even though it had not consciously registered with me. I didn't want to let the other women down or mess up their training, so I had told myself I needed to keep up no matter what. Even though I knew they would have been kind and slowed down, I didn't want to ask for this. After I came to this realization and had a conversation with my inner self, I was able to let that emotion pass through my body, and not surprisingly, the cramping stopped. My subconscious mind had used my physical body as a messenger.

Another time while dealing with a difficult situation with

someone I had an "aha" moment. I had been continually waking randomly with neck pain. I also had severe itching on my neck for several months. There are many really great books out there that outline what a particular ailment may be about emotionally, and in my experience, they are pretty spot on. I had read neck issues often show up when we are unwilling to look at the other side of an issue. I immediately admonished myself for this and felt like I clearly wasn't thinking of the other person in all of this...then suddenly it occurred to me that *all* I'd done was think of them in this. I'd held on and tried to continually help and make them feel comfortable when all the while, I'd ignored my own needs. I'd known how toxic it was for a long time, yet I had not told them because of how much they were struggling in their life at the time. Meanwhile, I was walking on eggshells and was constantly feeling stressed. I think the pain in my neck was my inner self crying out saying, "What about us?" Once I acknowledged this, and took action to change the situation, the discomfort and itching stopped.

For a period of several years, I had plantar fasciitis in both of my feet. It was excruciating. Every morning when I got out of bed, it felt like I was stepping on knives. I went to physical therapy, I tried stretching, icing, different braces, inserts in my shoes, and finally cortisone injections. Nothing helped. The podiatrist told me he believed the only thing that would likely help me was surgery. I didn't want surgery. At that time, I was new to emotional processing and didn't fully understand the mind/body connection, but I was beginning to. I kept trying to ask myself where this was coming from, and

I got the impression I was carrying a lot of fear, specifically around security. I began starting each day saying, "My body feels good, my feet feel good, I'm safe, and it will be a great day" before I took my first step out of bed. Each day I did this, the pain became less. It wasn't just about speaking the mantra I had created for myself, it was the awareness of the fear I was not acknowledging previously; which allowed me to question it and work through it. I no longer was expecting pain when my feet hit the floor, and eventually, it completely went away. I didn't end up having surgery, and it's never come back.

If you are experiencing pain or discomfort in any area of your body, take some time to sit down and close your eyes, allowing yourself to go inward. When we have our eyes closed, it helps us to shut out outside influences and really get in touch with our own inner world. Use this quiet opportunity to talk to your body. As crazy as it sounds, have a conversation with the part of your body that is hurting. So, if like I experienced, your feet are hurting, ask your feet, "Is there something I need to know or understand from this pain I am having?" Then listen for the response. You'll likely have a thought come to mind with an answer within. This is coming from your subconscious mind.

Once you receive an answer, you can then ask, "What do I need to do to clear this?" And again, a reply in the form of a thought will come to you. This may take some practice, and you must learn to trust the responses you get. We have all the answers to all the questions within our own mind, heart, and soul.

An example might be if you are having trouble clearing your throat, the response you get may be that you need to learn to use your voice, or to speak your mind in a situation. This is also a problem I used to have. I would lose my voice, or when I would speak, it would be so low no one would hear me. I did a lot of work on healing my past, and eventually, I realized I no longer feared saying what I needed to in order to protect myself or be authentic, and ever since then, my voice is much clearer and more confident.

Physical responses in the body are like the lights on the dashboard of our car. A light comes on to let us know there is an issue to be addressed. When we have an emotional issue, and especially if we are ignoring it, our body will respond with a physical signal for us. This is a powerful tool to have at our disposal. If you can recognize a physical problem as a light on your "dashboard," it's like having a secret door to solve a problem. Too often we are walking around knowing we have an issue to address but not knowing where to begin, so we will avoid and ignore it hoping it will just go away. But it won't. On the contrary, it will usually get more intense rather than go away.

With a little practice, you can get answers from your physical pain just like you can get answers from your emotions. When I notice a physical issue in my body, I recognize I need to start asking myself some questions. Most often, I can get to the root cause and find a resolution by processing my feelings. Because the emotions are likely creating the pain, you can speak to the feeling, or to the body part that is hurting.

Please note, I am not suggesting you forgo medical care if it is needed, I'm just suggesting sometimes we can help ourselves immensely by examining what we feel about something. It never hurts to open up to your feelings, in fact, the only time a feeling can hurt us is when we leave it unacknowledged.

 ## KEY FOR CHANGE

A great way to make that mind/body connection is to do a meditation where you are scanning your body one part at a time, noticing each part, and if there are any areas that seem to be holding tension, tightness, or pain, it's an opportunity to communicate with the subconscious messages held within the cells of your body. Imagine as you scan your body, areas that need attention from you light up in red. You can then speak directly to each body part that has lit up and ask what it is you need to know to find relief, improvement, or change. Notice as you scan your body again if the light has changed. If it hasn't, you may want to continue asking your body questions until the light has stopped being red.

CHAPTER 5

If I had a DeLorean

In the process of letting go, you will lose many things from the past, but you will find yourself

~ Deepak Chopra,

Transforming the World Through Open Minds and Hearts

In the 1985 movie, *Back to the Future*, Marty McFly uses a time machine made out of a DeLorean—a short lived sports car from the early 80's—as a way to go back and "correct" things from his parents' past that had affected him in his present life. What if we could do that? What if we could see where things went wrong in our history and go back to make changes? While we can't physically go back, nor can we change the reality of what occurred, we can follow our emotions back in time to where the initial events that hurt us came from, and process through them so that our perspective on them changes.

We don't want to live in the past, but sometimes it's important to revisit it for the purpose of finding peace and integrating the experiences we had into the present so that the future comes with ease. What we learn or experience in childhood becomes our operating system in adulthood, and in order to "update" our system, we need to explore the feelings from those events.

We won't change what happened, but changing what we feel will allow us to change what we think about those experiences, and in turn, so will the path of our life.

What does it mean to "revisit" the past? Well, I think it means we take a look at what happened, and instead of staying stuck in the emotions of the time, we look at what we learned and how it has changed us for the better. If something keeps coming up for you from your past, there's a good chance you need to let yourself really feel all of your feelings from the event completely.

When we go back and evaluate our experiences and really look into them and not just see how we were hurt, but look for understanding beneath the layers of emotions, we will find valuable insights, lessons, and most importantly, the truth. So often we allow our feelings to tell us a story that isn't entirely real, and we use that story to back up our thoughts which then define our behaviors and view of ourselves.

There is a type of hypnosis called regression hypnotherapy which I use with clients as a means to revisit the past. It involves taking an emotion we feel and following it back to the first time we ever felt it. If something happens when we are a child that makes us feel afraid but because we are so young, we don't have the tools to really express that fear, we kind of tuck it away, or if you want to imagine it like placing a brick on a wall. The next time we experience that same fearful feeling and if again we don't know how to work through it, another brick is placed. This process will continue on until our stack of bricks is quite tall, figuratively building an "emotional wall."

Eventually, that original feeling is likely to be triggered again and again, and now because there has been so much weight added to it, it's not just uncomfortable but is maybe a primary driving emotion in our life. The brick wall we have built may be so tall and strong it's impenetrable...we can't see over it, under it, or around it. It's like we just keep staring at it and the story we've written on it, and we read it over and over again.

I was working with a woman who had extreme health anxiety. She was constantly googling symptoms over every little thing she noticed that was "off" in her body. A spot on her face, a pain in her back, a returning headache. She kept believing she had or would have cancer and might die. It was stealing her joy. She was unable to fully appreciate the goodness in her life and really live. She had a child and that seemed to make the health anxiety worse. She was in fear every day she would leave her daughter without a mother. We had to go back to the past, where we visited a memory of her mom being diagnosed with an aggressive cancer. Her mom ended up passing away, and then a few years later, a second mother figure in her life also got cancer, and she too did not survive.

My client had a belief that not only did her mother figures get cancer and die, but they didn't take care of themselves because she wasn't worth fighting or living for.

We followed her fear back to when her mom got sick, and she had some revelations. There's always more truth in a memory than we are able to see at first glance. By first glance, I mean the feeling that brought us there to begin with. She believed because she saw two women she loved get cancer, it was only a matter of time until she did. There was a part of her that believed they chose to leave her. Her adult mind could see they didn't actually want that, but rather the circumstance was out of their control; it was the child inside who had the original emotions, that didn't understand this. When going back to the memory, she was able to see they very much loved her and wanted to be there for her.

She had been living in fear she also would get cancer, die, and leave her child without a mother. Her powerful emotions had not been processed from her youth and created a story she was just waiting to have play out. Her unresolved feelings from the past were ruling her life in her present. By going back to the memory, she was able to talk to her younger self and provide the answers no one was able to for her back then. She saw her mother had some cultural influences from her own upbringing that prevented her from seeking medical care soon enough. She also saw her mom had a toughness and fighting spirit within her that she herself felt she inherited from her, and she now believed had her mom felt worthy of getting appropriate medical care and had sought help early on, she might have survived. Most importantly, she saw she was worthy of her mom living for and it wasn't about her.

After processing her fear from decades before and in essence getting the first brick from the pile, she was able to knock down that wall of fear and find relief and changes to her current understanding and belief. She no longer saw every little thing as an indicator of inevitable death. She was free from that idea and could now see other possibilities.

Imagine a baby bird cracking out of its shell. This bird has a tiny, temporary tooth on her beak called an egg tooth. It is there just to help her get out of her shell. She will use it to get to the next stage in her life. Consider how many things in life come along to help us move from one situation to another, just like this egg tooth. Going back to process emotions of past events can be like this shell cracking tooth. I remember when I first started doing hypnotherapy sessions with my mentor to work on my own healing. After every session, I would say to him, "That's it! That's what I've needed all along." I had some misguided perception I'd suddenly found all the answers I'd been looking for, and now I would get to move into some per-fectly peaceful life, and I'd somehow "made it" through it all. It was like I thought I'd cracked through this shell that was holding me in, and now I'd have it all solved.

He would just smile and nod, and somehow, I knew he knew something I didn't. And of course, he did. He knew there was no real finish line to the process of healing, or being born (or hatched as in the case of our little bird) as I like to think of it. He knew even though the work we had just done was going to make a profound difference in my life and I had surely cracked through one layer, it wasn't going to sud-denly change *everything*. This was true, but in some ways, it wasn't. Every session and every revelation brought me to a greater understanding of myself. It opened the door a little wider and let in a touch more light. Over time, doing these sessions, things changed for me in ways I never thought possible. I started to feel less burdened, I felt a greater acceptance of myself and, in turn, of others. Judgment fell away, peace did indeed step in. Was everything perfect? Nope. But what had happened was in learning to know myself, I learned better ways to deal with the world around me. Doing those sessions was like finding my egg tooth. I'd cracked through a lot of things that had been keeping me stuck, frozen, sad, lost, and confused. It was a valuable tool for that stage of my healing, and one I still use, but I'm no longer naive enough to believe there won't be more work to do in the days to come. I understand this now, because I know "healing" is really a lifelong journey. There will always be more to heal as I get to know myself better and meet my own dark places. My egg tooth may come and go, but I know I will have it when I need it. For every new tool I can put in my healing toolbox, there will be another layer uncovered, processed, and resolved.

I've learned to have more grace for myself as the days pass, knowing in this life there is no perfection. There is no completion with healing. There is only a continuance of doing the best I can every day, and this is what we can all ultimately strive for.

Did you know grasshoppers can only move forward? They cannot go backward or even side to side, sometimes they make little hops and sometimes they propel themselves forward with great force and even can fly. But they cannot go in reverse. Be like a grasshopper, move forward. So, while processing past events is powerful and often necessary, staying stuck in past events makes it so you keep on repeating the same story over and over. The characters in the story may be different, and sometimes the scenes in the story change, but the emotions will play out again and again and will continue to do so until the original hurt is healed.

So, yes, go back, but then make the choice to leap forward.

Going back to the past is beneficial if we use it in this way, if our intention is to not stay there in a negative way, but rather gather information and move ourselves ahead. While we may need to revisit the past to get clarity, we do not want to stay stuck there. We want to process what's there so that our feelings can change, and then so we can create new and better thoughts about what we experienced.

A magical thing happens when we change, those we associate with begin to change too. One person can start a revolution… no matter how small. It can be within our own household, or our social circle, within our extended family, or even our community. It's like dominoes. One touches another and it falls, or in the case of growth, one touches another, and a seed is planted in the mind, indeed in the very soul of the person. They may not change immediately, but over time, if they continue to see another being self-aware and working hard to change themselves for the better, they will want that too. Good things are contagious. It's like seeing someone thoroughly enjoying an ice cream sundae, it makes us hungry for that as well.

When we go to those past events that have us stuck in a loop of believing things like "I am not worthy," or that "My life is just hard," or "I'll never get ahead," we can find the truth, and the truth is we ARE worthy. What challenges us, indeed changes us, and we can move as far ahead as our dreams carry us, we only have to be willing.

When practicing yoga, at first a pose or stretch might feel hard, or even impossible, but then we take a deep breath, and on the next try, the stretch is a bit further, and with each subsequent breath, it's further still. Healing happens in layers just like stretching.

Pushing just a little further or a little harder is sometimes all it takes to move to the next level. Is it uncomfortable? Absolutely, but growth of any kind usually is.

This applies to all of life, pushing a little harder or a little further can leave us feeling challenged and wondering if we are able to do it, but in the end, you don't know until you try, and when you do, the reward is greater than the pain endured. Try to remember, healing isn't going to be without pain. Looking back over difficult situations is likely to hurt, but something wonderful happens when you allow your subconscious mind to speak to you, to bring to the surface what has been making you uncomfortable, and instead of ignoring it, you integrate what you have learned from it and become a better, stronger, happier you.

We all have traumas and challenges from our past. It's inevitable. Those experiences are part of what shapes who we are and how we respond to things. The first time we feel a particular feeling in life, it leaves a mark on our subconscious that gets filed away. The next time we feel that same feeling even if the circumstances are different, it will make that original feeling more intense. Likewise, every subsequent event with that emotion makes that pile a little bigger. Eventually, that original emotion is likely to feel a little overwhelming. If we can go back using the access point of our subconscious mind, we can process that first feeling, and in doing so, it will make the intensity of the other times we felt that emotion a little less or sometimes it will make them ease entirely.

Think of it this way. You have a bucket of clear water. One day, something really hurts you, and that feeling of hurt adds a drop of blue to the water. The water is now a light blue color. If you don't do anything with that first hurt feeling, the water stays that same color blue. However, if you are hurt again and don't process the feeling this time either, another droplet of blue is added. Now the bucket of water is an even darker blue. The water will become more and more blue with every time you experience that same emotion and don't do anything to help yourself process the feelings. Yet, if you take the time to begin working through those painful feelings, the blue water gets lighter and lighter until eventually it is clear again. Clarity is the goal. When we have clear thinking, we can make good choices for our own well-being as well as those around us.

I saw a post on Facebook a couple years ago that has stayed with me. Someone was talking about a scar they have, and they said how it was a reminder of something hard they had gone through. They asked for others to show their scars. It was interesting because a lot of scar photos started appearing in the comments, but then there were words. Lots of words. Stories of scars on their hearts, on their very souls that were not visible, yet shaped who they were and gave them qualities like resiliency, strength, problem solving skills, and yes, even hope.

Go back to what hurt you and confront it head on, but go with the intention of removing the bricks from the wall, or making the bucket of water clear again. Freeing yourself from old hurts is better than allowing yourself to revel in validation for your pain. You won't grow from that.

KEY FOR CHANGE

Sometimes we need to revisit the past in order to adequately process our feelings about painful or traumatic events.

You may know of something that was a defining painful experience in your past, or you may have some events you know were painful, but you haven't actively associated with current issues in your life.

Take a moment, eyes closed; again, this is the easiest way to access your subconscious mind and ask, "Is there an event in my past that is affecting me today?"

See what comes up.

Changing your perspective from thinking things that happened in your past happened to you to seeing how they happened for you to grow and learn will assist you in moving forward with goals, dreams, and meeting your true self.

If there is something particularly painful in your past you feel you can't work through on your own, be sure to reach out to a therapist and let them walk with you as you move toward the truth.

CHAPTER 6

WHO IS THIS INNER CHILD?

Hello inner child, I'm the inner babysitter

~ Terry Pratchett, *Hogfather*

This quote is a little funny, but at the same time holds truth. We ourselves are the one looking out for our inner child, and if we are not, we need to be. We have the opportunity every day to in essence "re-parent" the child within us. I'm sure you've heard people talk about "inner child" work, but do you know what that means? Just who is this "inner child" we are supposed to work with, and why?

Our inner child is part of our subconscious mind. It's our beliefs, emotions, and memories, as well as our hopes and dreams for the future. It's creative and spontaneous, and it's every version of you, every age of you, that you have ever been. An effective part of healing is working with this part of your subconscious. As I said earlier, it's so important to process your emotions and let yourself really feel whatever it is you need to from past experiences. Feeling these emotions and connecting with the "you" that first felt them is a place where powerful and profound healing happens. The first step is acknowledging this part of you exists.

There is a child inside us all who is looking for attention and validation in the world, and the first place that child needs to receive those things is from the adult who is carrying the child within. When that child doesn't feel loved, he or she begins to act out, much like an actual child would. The inner child seeks our attention and will try many different things to gain it. This may show up as the earlier discussed physical pain, emotional overwhelm, addictive habits, destructive behaviors, self-sabotage, and more.

Because your inner child lives in your subconscious, connecting is as easy as deciding you want to. There are many ways to do this, but a simple way is again to first close your eyes, and then begin to see in your mind's eye a younger you. Talking to your inner child works the same as previously mentioned to connect with your subconscious mind in general. To start, I like to suggest a five-or six-year-old you. If you can't remember what you looked like, maybe find a picture of your younger self and use that to help you get started. Why five or six years old? Well, from the age of zero to five is typically when your view of yourself and the world around you is formed. The information creating that view comes from authority figures in your life. Your parents, grandparents, teachers, and even older siblings. Your young brain is absorbing everything you hear and see and is taking its cues from those experiences.

Those other versions of you may not have had the

opportunity to be heard, to say what they needed to, or to receive the message that would help them get through the difficult time when it happened. As a result, trauma can be stored, and as a way to protect oneself, unhealthy coping mechanisms will be employed to suppress or avoid facing those difficult memories.

Giving your inner child the chance to speak and be heard while the adult you responds with the needed message will assist you in moving forward. So, what does this mean exactly?

If I'm working with someone and they go back to a painful memory, for example witnessing a violent act and being afraid to do something to help (which is absolutely the appropriate response for a child), but as an adult, they have held themselves responsible for that and can't seem to let go of the idea they should have done something, I would have them imagine they were present with the child version of themselves and view the situation with adult understanding. Then I would ask them to talk to the child version of themselves and let the child tell them how they are feeling and provide the response the child needed at that time but was unavailable to them. It may have been unavailable because no adult was present or because the adults present were involved in the traumatic event and were not capable of responding. By doing so, the adult version of themselves is providing what the child needed and didn't receive at the time of the original event, which will help them release the responsibility for something they had no control over.

This is not to lay blame on your parents, they were doing the best they could at the time with where they were on their own emotional journey. It's really what we are all doing all the time. We all have knowledge and understanding that is continually growing and changing, and we respond as we are capable in that moment. While it isn't about blame, it's obviously not an excuse for someone hurting you either, but it is a statement of truth. The best one person can do in a moment may be miles away from the best another can do.

Some signs your inner child may possibly need some attention from you are:

- Overreacting to small things with very big emotions
- Struggling with self-esteem
- Self-sabotaging
- Having difficulties with relationships
- Experiencing physical or mental issues
- Employing unhealthy coping mechanisms

When we heal our inner child, we heal our adult self.

Things to say to your inner child to help him or her be comforted are:

- "I see you and love you."
- "Is there something you need to tell me?"
- "It's ok that you want things to be different."
- "You did all you could do."
- "Your feelings matter and are valid."
- "You are perfect just as you are."

- "You can be yourself."
- "The things that happened to you were not your fault."
- "You are good enough already."
- "It's safe to feel your feelings."

It's also important to praise your inner child when he or she has done well at something. We are always quick to scold or berate ourselves, but loving praise is very important. When you've worked hard on something and even if it doesn't go the way you wanted it to, saying something kind and loving to acknowledge your effort will help you combat a possible fear of failing if you try again. After a long day, take a moment to find something good you have done and give yourself (and that inner child who just wants to be loved) a compliment.

KEY FOR CHANGE

Here's a meditation that is easy and fun to do that will help you connect with your inner child (which can be you at any age you have ever been) and also provide an opportunity to process some past emotions. When I do this meditation, I like to imagine I am sitting under a tree in my backyard where I grew up. As I'm sitting there, I ask every age I have ever been to come and sit with me. Soon I see various ages of myself coming and joining me on the grass. I'll see an eight-year-old me riding up on my bicycle that had the sparkly blue banana seat, a teenage me in my favorite brown leather jacket carrying a one-year-old me with my favorite toy, all of the 20's, 30's, and 40's versions of me and so on coming along and being present with me. (Some of us will have a bigger crowd than others!) Then, I will ask, is there any version of me here who has something she needs to say or be heard about? I'll then wait for different ages to stand, then I will ask them what I need to know to help them feel better. It's really powerful.

You could do this every day to gradually work through whatever is on your list of things in need of healing.

Another way to connect to your inner child is through play. Remembering and doing things you enjoyed as a kid will help you make that connection to him or her. One early morning recently my friend Erin and I were returning from a run, and we ended at a local park. As we ran into the parking lot, I looked over and saw the playground equipment. I turned and looked at her and said, "Do you wanna go swing?" She quickly exclaimed "Yes!" Soon we were swinging high, feet in the air, laughing (which was quickly followed by feeling nauseous—hey, we aren't physically as young as we once were, though our hearts enjoyed the play). Later that day, she sent me a text saying how she couldn't stop smiling. I responded with "me too." It's good to remember the joy of childhood. Try riding a bike, running through the grass, drawing, coloring, blowing bubbles, or playing a game. Remembering how to have fun is healing in and of itself. We can't be serious all the time.

CHAPTER 7

Forgive Your Way to Freedom

There is no love without forgiveness and there is no forgiveness without love.

~Bryant H. McGill, *Facebook, July 11, 2014*

What does it mean to forgive someone? Forgiveness is an intentional decision to let go of anger and resentment. It is an act of love for others, but most importantly for ourselves. When we choose to not forgive…and it is a choice, we are in essence poisoning ourselves. We are doing greater damage than the person who hurt us in the first place may have done. That non-forgiveness plays the hurt out over and over again. Each time we recall the hurt, it digs in a little deeper. To quote Marianne Williamson, "Not forgiving someone is like drinking poison and waiting for the other person to die."

The other person won't die of course, they won't even know if we are harboring ill feelings toward them in most cases. But we, ourselves will be dying a little inside each time we think of our anger. Our negative thoughts and emotions do indeed play a big part in our health and well-being. It helps sometimes to think of it not as "forgiving" which might cause you to feel it's for the other person more than for you, but rather framing it as simply "letting go."

If the idea of forgiving makes you picture handing a gift to an undeserving recipient, perhaps instead imagine you are holding a balloon with the negative experiences and feelings you've had with someone, and while you are holding it, it pulls you along with it, taking it wherever it feels like going. If you can untie the tether and let it float off and allow yourself to feel the freedom of release, it might make the concept of forgiveness easier to bear. You are letting go of the hurt, while being the one to make the conscious decision to do so, after your subconscious and you process and reframe your feelings about the person and/or situation. It doesn't mean you have to keep the person in your life, it just means you won't be negatively connected to them.

Do you have a favorite movie you have watched many times in your life? If the answer is yes, think about that movie. Can you quickly recall favorite lines? How about details of the actors? How does that movie make you feel when you watch it? When we continue to replay a painful situation over and over, it's like watching a movie again and again. The more you watch, the more you remember, the more you identify with it, and the more a part of you it becomes. Remember your favorite movie again. Has that movie been your favorite for a long time? Do you change favorites frequently, or do you fall back to that old most memorable one?

This is what we do with our hurts. We will keep replaying those old transgressions and feeling wounded again and again until it is second nature to us. We become less and less willing to let it go because we begin to feel like we are owed some kind of grand gesture in reparation. In the end, it's finding some empathy and understanding that will be the thing we need most. Yes, an apology is always welcome, but the apology alone is not going to make it so we can move forward. Action on our own part is required.

Not forgiving someone can make us think we have "won" or are in control of the situation. The opposite is true. We are losing with every second we harbor bitterness and resentment. We are not in control; we are in fact being controlled. Controlled by the negative feelings. Allowing ourselves to keep feeling the pain is like being punished for a crime we didn't commit. You are sending your innocent self to an eternal jail to be tortured day after day. With forgiveness comes freedom. Of course, it's not as simple as just saying you forgive someone, you must truly want to release the hurt before you can fly freely from your cage.

But how do we do that when we have been wronged? How can we see someone as worthy of forgiveness if they have seemingly acted in a hateful way with no regard for our feelings? When we have been hurt, forgiving can be the most challenging thing to do. Some people might ask why does it matter anyway if we forgive someone or not? The energy of non-forgiveness stays stuck in your body and can create lots of problems. Some of them are emotional problems, like having difficulty trusting people, or letting others get close to you. Some of them can be physical problems because we know our mind and body are so connected.

Imagine for a moment you are carrying a very heavy box, and you are gripping onto it so tightly that your arms begin to shake and your hands ache. Inside the box is the pain a person has caused you. The thing is the person who hurt you has no idea you are holding this box. They are not feeling the strain of your muscles or the weight of the contents. They have no idea. It's not about giving them relief, it's about giving *you* relief. Processing your feelings about a person or situation allows you to release your grip on the box, set it down, and step away from it.

Sometimes we need to take a good look at the person who hurt us to try and understand what might have caused them to have this behavior toward us. What is it in them that is hurting that made them lash out or do something thoughtless or insensitive toward us? Do they feel confident, secure, and good enough, or are those things lacking in them? Finding empathy for the one who wounded us can be very helpful. It doesn't excuse the behavior, but rather it might give us a new perspective as to the cause of their actions which will serve to help us see that we didn't do anything wrong or deserve the treatment we received.

It can help, too, if we put ourselves in the other person's shoes. This is most effective if the person has actually offered a sincere apology to you. If we can imagine or remember a time we acted in a way we were not proud of and how that affected someone else, we may find it easier to open up to releasing. Remembering how much we wanted to be forgiven can help us be gentler toward the person who hurt us, and in turn, toward ourselves if we remember we are the one hurt most deeply by being unforgiving.

I had a client who unknowingly stored anger in her body for a very long time. She had struggled with men in her life in various relationships over the years and didn't realize she was subconsciously very angry toward them. She was always walking around "being positive" and denying herself that anger. She was also continually having UTIs and kidney infections. We worked on releasing this anger by confronting the painful memories from her past. In a session, she had a realization that the kidney issues were being caused by this anger she was harboring. She was quite literally "pissed off."

Anger can be a very strong emotion, and it's often helpful to move the body as the feelings and memories are coming up. Holding a pillow on your lap and saying what you are angry about while moving your fists into the pillow can be tremendously healing. When the movement of your arms and the force of the blows slows and the angry emotion is expended, the energy behind it runs out. At this point, clarity can come.

My client used her fists to move the feelings from her physical body to the outside. As she punched, she wasn't envisioning punching the offenders, but she was releasing the emotion from their actions. She was using phrases like "I'm so angry that you betrayed me" and "I'm so angry that you were never there for me." Going through one painful experience with men after another starting with her father, then a boyfriend, and a husband she had divorced. With every angry statement she verbalized, I watched her posture improve, and her dignity and poise returned.

We might walk around feeling all these angry thoughts but think it makes us a bad person because we have them. So, rather than confronting the feelings head on, we pretend they aren't there and instead hold onto non-forgiveness like it gives us the power over the other person. It's a truly beautiful moment watching someone realize they had been holding the key to their own cage all along.

With this client, after she processed all of the long-standing anger, her health improved. She reported back as I was writing this that she had not had another UTI or kidney infection in the four years since doing that particular session. She gained an understanding that the people themselves were not bad, they just were not capable at that time of doing things any differently than they had. She made the choice to let go of the pain and freed herself. She validated her own feelings, allowing herself to truly feel them and acknowledge she was justified in having them, but also realizing she didn't have to be controlled by them.

Her subconscious needed to be heard. Something shifted for her. She felt the power of forgiveness, and a new understanding came over her. She knew then the other people weren't even aware of her non-forgiveness, and she herself was the only one suffering.

For a long time, I thought I had to "forgive and forget," but in reality, what I thought I had to do was pretend it never happened and just deal with it. There was no freedom in that choice, because as I grew to understand, I wasn't really forgiving or letting go of anything. I was avoiding it altogether. I was denying forgiveness and instead, putting blinders on, excusing poor behavior in an attempt to be righteous. I was denying my feelings of anger, of hurt, and of sadness because I was still in my old belief of always accepting any behavior by someone else no matter how it made me feel, because I was not honoring myself or seeing my own worth. This led me into so many codependent relationships, romantic and otherwise. It was almost as if I was allowing myself to be a vessel for other people's anguish and unhealed emotions. It was like I had a sign on my forehead that said, "It's ok for you to dump your pain on me, it's my job to carry it." Ugh. I still cringe when I think of that. I've become so much more skilled at noticing codependent behavior at the onset. I am no longer willing to be a life raft, but I'm happy to teach someone how to swim.

So, how do we find forgiveness or the ability to let go when someone has hurt us?

Recently, I was working with a client, and at the end of the session, she asked why I didn't have her say she forgave the person she had been upset with. I told her I couldn't make her do that, but I felt she had organically forgiven because as we worked through the event, when I asked how she felt about the person, she said she felt compassion and empathy. She didn't have to come right out and say she had found forgiveness. We can say we forgive all day long, but the words don't mean anything without the feeling. I could tell she authentically was able to release the hurt and therefore I didn't need to ask.

Forgiveness is not just a set of words, it's a true understanding we can see the human qualities in the other person and where their internal pain that may have caused them to act negatively in the first place had come from. In the end, forgiveness is a gift to oneself. It is an act of higher love. We don't deserve to be held in a cage from our inability to forgive. We've already been hurt, releasing the negative feelings frees us. Remember, it's letting go of the negative emotions about the person or event, not dismissing the action, or even allowing the person to remain in your life. It's still important to have appropriate boundaries with the offender, which may mean not seeing them. It's a release for you, and it's your choice where you go from there.

KEY FOR CHANGE

Non-forgiveness doesn't hurt the person who we need to forgive, it hurts us. Withholding forgiveness can affect your mental and physical health and well-being.

In order to forgive, we must first process our feelings about what it is we are not finding forgiveness for.

Taking time to look at the other person and see why they may have behaved the way they did will allow us to have empathy and compassion, which is what we need in order to truly forgive.

Is there someone in your life you are finding it hard to forgive?

Are you ready to acknowledge your emotions about that hurt and see if you can find the higher love that will free you?

Take some time asking yourself these questions and deciding whether you want to make the choice to forgive.

A way to work toward forgiveness is to imagine you are sitting across the table from someone who has hurt you. In this vision, they are not able to speak, you are going to look into their eyes, the proverbial window into the soul. You will look at them and see if you can understand why they did or said what they did. Where is this coming from for them?

Most often, you will see there is a lack of self-worth, a feeling of not being good enough, no confidence, sadness, and or wounding from their own past experiences (you may or may not know about their past, but you will get a sense of it as you look at them). Once you see what they are missing, you can choose to give them a blessing if you feel ready to do so. What I like to do is look at what they would have needed to respond to you in a better way in the first place. If it's self-worth, I would say, "May you be blessed with more self-worth than ever before" and taking a deep breath imagine that as I exhale, they receive the blessing. It's tremendously freeing for the person giving the blessing, and the energy of love will go to the other person wherever they are. They won't know what you have done, but their energy will receive it. This exercise frees you as you find compassion and empathy for the one who hurt you.

Offering a blessing to them is also blessing you, forgiveness is freedom.

Pardon Me?

Sometimes we find it is far easier to forgive others than it is to forgive ourselves. We are often quick to offer pardon to those who have hurt us yet hold ourselves to an almost impossible standard. We will be consumed by feelings of guilt and punish ourselves over and over. Is there anything in your past you find difficult to forgive yourself for? If so, ask yourself a few questions. "Am I punishing myself too much for something I did or said when I just didn't know better?" "Do I deserve to suffer for this mistake forever?" You might also ask "Am I not forgiving myself for something I didn't even do, but my mind perceives guilt for anyway?" These questions will assist you in beginning to find the path to self-forgiveness.

I had an experience with someone in my life I was constantly looking for approval from, only to be hurt and feel rejected time after time. I'd find myself feeling guilty when I considered pulling away all together. I'd chastise myself for not trying hard enough. I kept thinking sooner or later, the person would begin to invest in the relationship in the same way I had. Sadly, they never did. There were a few times over the years I thought maybe they were going to start putting some effort out, but I eventually grew to understand they were just not capable of giving anything more to the relationship.

This experience left me with self-doubt and a feeling of unworthiness for a long time. I'd say I'd let it go, but then find myself right back to questioning my wrongdoing in the situation. I felt so much guilt but had a turning point when I realized I needed to grieve the idea of what I had wanted the relationship to be. I had not actually lost the relationship, that still existed in its dysfunctional way, but I had lost what I desired in that particular relationship. Once I came to this understanding, something shifted. I began to release myself from obligation. I had been giving and giving with nothing in return. In fact, I started noticing a pattern where in interactions with the person, they never once asked anything about what was going on in my life. They only talked about themselves and continually turned things in their direction, expecting me to carry the full weight of keeping any connection with them. Recognizing I had not been able to forgive myself for the things that were missing, I now could see clearly I had not done anything wrong in wanting a connection with them, and I realized I couldn't change they didn't want that, or maybe more than that, were not capable of it. I finally felt I could forgive myself, not for not making the relationship work, but for thinking I had to. I was able to stop blaming myself for this when I confronted my emotions about it and the other person, and allowed myself to see the truth, not a clouded version of the truth.

I had a client who couldn't move past the grief of losing her parents. They both passed at different times, and both were natural causes in old age. It seemed she felt responsible for keeping their memory alive, and it almost consumed her. She was so focused on keeping their house and their possessions to the point she was not leaving space to live her own life. She didn't feel she could change the decor in their home (her home by then) or get rid of anything that was theirs. It was almost as if she expected them to walk back in the front door one day. We worked really hard on processing grief, and coming to an understanding grief was an indicator of the great love she had for them, yet she still struggled to move on. Eventually, it clicked that she needed to forgive herself for all she thought she had not done for them, and for any moments she had missed with them. Soon, she was able to begin sorting through their things and keeping a few mementos but parting with many other things. Finally, she was able to sell their home and buy her own house, a place she filled with her things and began truly living her own life. Forgiving herself was instrumental in creating space emotionally for this to happen.

Another client was struggling with infertility. She had two children but longed for one more. She had suffered multiple miscarriages that were traumatic for her. She was blaming herself for not being able to get pregnant and for losing the pregnancies she did have. I could feel the weight of her emotions around this subject and how much responsibility she was taking for all of it. She was unable to forgive herself even though it obviously was not something she wanted, and she had in fact been doing everything right. We had a powerful session where we processed her emotions around her pregnancy loses, and she came to a clear place of forgiveness for herself. Within two months, she was pregnant, and in nine months after that, delivered a healthy baby.

When we withhold forgiveness of ourselves, we are the one locking the cage door tightly closed. No one is doing this to us, we are the one with the power to open that door. Are there things in your life you are not forgiving yourself for?

If so, ask yourself a few questions. "Have I done something wrong?" If the answer to that is yes, try to remember we are human, we are going to make mistakes and hurt others sometimes, but we can't stay locked in that event. We must unpack it and our feelings about it so we can progress. If we punish ourselves over and over, we are going to stay stuck. A better option is to think of yourself like you would someone else. If a friend hurt you, would you withhold forgiveness if a sincere apology was offered? (I understand sometimes you may not want to continue in that friendship, depending on the circumstances, but hopefully, you can still come to a place of letting go—as discussed in the previous section.)

We are all worthy and deserving of forgiving grace. All of us, even you.

KEY FOR CHANGE

It helps to look at what you have learned from the experience you are struggling to forgive yourself for. If we see the event can come with something positive gained, releasing yourself from the hold of guilt will come easier.

You are worthy of the same forgiveness you would offer to another person. Try to think of it that way if you are having a hard time offering yourself forgiveness.

Also ask yourself what you would have needed to behave differently in the first place. For example, would I have been kinder to the person I hurt if I had healthy self-esteem? Knowing what you would have needed will not only assist you in not repeating the behavior, but it will give you insight into what you might need to work on within yourself. Let grace replace guilt.

Remember, too, sometimes we are blaming and withholding forgiveness of ourselves for something we didn't even do, so be sure to ask yourself "Did I actually do something wrong in this situation?"

Looking inward and processing your feelings about events will help you release yourself and move forward.

CHAPTER 8

NOT A TRAGEDY, BUT AN OPPORTUNITY

There are always flowers
for those who want to see them.

~Henri Matisse, *Jazz*

I've had some difficult and painful experiences in my life, as we all have. I may have wished things would be different in many instances, but at the same time, I have learned to love and appreciate each and every one of those painful experiences, because they helped me grow. I didn't always see it that way though.

Sixteen years ago, I went to see an acupuncturist for the first time. I was hoping she could help me with an injury to my foot, but in addition, I was struggling emotionally as well. I remember sharing some painful things I was dealing with in my life at that time. My marriage was struggling, I felt unsatisfied in my career, I was teetering on the edge of an eating disorder, and generally felt like I'd lost my way. I remember this quiet, beautiful soul telling me this, "Try not to look at this as a tragedy, but rather as an opportunity."

It was many years before I really knew what she meant.

When she first said it, I was very much in victim mode. Always believing things were stacked against me, everyone was trying to hurt me, life was unfair, and I would never really get to be happy. How was all my pain an opportunity?

That phrase sat in the back of my mind for years, always replaying when things were hard, and even though I didn't fully understand what she was trying to say to me, my mind took me back to those words. Then, one day when I started really processing the emotions I had about the events in my life, it hit me what she meant was every painful experience gives us an opportunity to find blessings in the challenges, and when we can do that, that is when we grow.

Instead of being angry and hurt, I started being grateful. I would send blessings to the person who had wronged me like, "Thank you for creating this painful experience for me, it helped me see where I needed to look inward and investigate where I need to change." I would try to take a step back when something challenged me and see if there was a lesson I was missing. If you have played a part in my story, that created pain for me at the time, I am not angry, I do not harbor hate for you. On the contrary, I thank you for making me stretch in this way. I thank you for being a part of my growth, and for being a catalyst for change.

A note to everyone though, just because you can see the blessings in a difficult situation you may have had with someone, does not give them license to remain in your life if they have not committed to making changes. It's important to still keep your boundaries and be sure you are honoring what is best for you.

I have worked with many people who have experienced trauma after trauma in their lives, and I have seen some of those people end up being the most well-adjusted, well-rounded, driven, and happy people. Why is that? I think the answer is simple, through all of the struggles, they have learned what is most important, and they have found the blessings in those situations that brought them pain. Indeed, they have seen them as opportunity rather than tragedy. They found gratitude for what they do have rather than focusing on what they don't have.

We have a choice in everything, we can choose to stay small, or we can choose to rise to the top, to break through all ceilings, to have everything we have ever wanted and more. This comes through being grateful which in turn opens possibilities in our lives. The more grateful we are, the more doors open for us. When we shut down and stay stuck in victimhood, we are unable to express gratitude, and that perpetuates the cycle of pain for us. To stop the cycle, give thanks and begin to see the opportunities in front of you.

So, how do you find a blessing in something that has hurt you? To begin with, again, you need to examine and process your feelings about the situation. This in and of itself will help you. If, for example, you were in an abusive relationship, taking time to process your feelings after the relationship ends will help. At this point, you will likely discover something like the fact you have found strength you didn't know you had, or insight about what you really want in life, that you may not have been aware of before or that you still wouldn't if you had stayed in the relationship in the first place.

Something to remember is when someone has hurt us, it isn't about us, it is about what they are feeling and experiencing, as well as how they likely feel about themselves. People will act out toward others in an attempt to soothe their own pain. This sounds so illogical, like how would hurting someone else make someone feel better.

I have used the analogy of someone carrying a very heavy suitcase and it's making them uncomfortable to carry, so they try to give it to you to get some relief. Instead of you taking it from them and lightening their load, the weight of it doubles. They still have to carry it, and as they tried to give it to you (through abuse and mistreatment), you may now have your own suitcase of pain to carry as well.

A better approach when someone tries to do that is instead of taking it from them, work to unpack it with them if they are willing. However, not everyone is ready for that, and in that case, you can send them blessings, create a boundary, and protect yourself from further hurts. This may mean ending a relationship whether it's romantic, family, or friendship. You can then look for the lessons, blessings, and growth that came from the experience.

KEY FOR CHANGE

Finding blessings in a situation can be a helpful way to move past something that has been difficult. If we can find something good even when things are not going our way, we can begin to shift the situation.

Is there something difficult you have experienced and have found challenging to move past? Write down what that event was and begin looking for something good that came from it. It may end up being you discovered your voice and expressed your needs, or you figured out something you do or don't want in future relationships.

Gratitude journals are talked about often in many different ways to help people see all of the good around them. Here's a little twist on a gratitude journal for you. If a normal gratitude journal would be writing down things you are grateful for each day, try creating an album on your phone's camera and start taking photos of things you are grateful for. When life becomes difficult or you are having a bad day, you can have a visual reminder of all of the good you have! Just seeing photos of your loved ones, pets, special places, quiet, and beautiful moments will impact your brain and create positive feelings.

CHAPTER 9

LOVE THE ONE IN THE MIRROR

"You have been criticizing yourself for years, and it hasn't worked. Try approving of yourself and see what happens."

— Louise Hay, *You Can Heal Your Life*

Love comes through acceptance, understanding, and releasing judgment. Self-love does too. It's where we all must start.

It was a warm day in October 2008, and I was sitting on the concrete curb outside a Washington DC metro station. I was completely depleted, exhausted, and in extreme pain. I couldn't muster the strength to enter the subway to get a train back to my car. The question running through my mind was "What am I doing?" I was so tired, every part of my body hurt. I had been punishing myself for over a year with excess exercise and restrictive eating, having a goal to run a marathon but not really sure why I wanted to do it. In the end, I don't think it had as much to do with wanting to run 26.2

miles as it had to do with numbing myself from pain I had stuffed down and avoided all my life.

My sense of unworthiness ran deep, and I always felt like something was wrong with me. Running was a distraction that enabled me to avoid dealing with the difficult emotions. Then I found if I ran even more and ate even less, I began to get smaller and smaller. I was already a petite woman at 5'4" and 115 pounds, but after a while, it became a quest of mine to shrink further. This mindset paralleled much of my way of thinking from my childhood. While my mom was always there for me and I was grateful for that, there was a period of time where my home life was often unstable and I was always trying to blend in, to be quiet, to not need anything. When I was a child, I didn't realize I was doing this, but I can see this now in looking back. At school, I was shy and unsure of my-self. I always had these deep emotions but had no idea what to do with them, so I simply avoided them. For some reason, I had convinced myself it was admirable to not have needs, to be small both in size and in personality. I held my cards close and struggled with letting others in.

I had started running in my teens just because I enjoyed it. Eventually, I went from running for fun to running as a way of destroying myself. I can see now it was because I just didn't know how to feel my feelings or see my own worth. Thus, the more I ran, the more I could forget these things. I began lim-iting my calories and running more and more miles. I would eat the lowest calorie foods and put them in small containers, so it looked like a lot of food to keep people from questioning me. Every pound the scale dropped was a victory. I felt like

I was accomplishing something. But all I was achieving was a slow path to destruction. At some point, something clicked in my mind that made me know it wasn't right, but by then, I couldn't seem to stop myself from running ten or more miles every day, which was way more than was needed to train for a marathon. I was eating only around 500 calories daily. The scale dropped more and more. At ninety-four pounds and a size zero being too large, I knew without a doubt I had a serious issue, though I still denied it to everyone who asked. I lied to my mom, my doctor, and my friends.

Thankfully, I did finally find my way out. It was a process, but I needed to start acknowledging my feelings. I needed to begin asking myself what my needs and desires were, and more than that, I needed to learn that I, as a person, had value. It was time to understand I was worthy and learn how to love and appreciate myself. I needed to unlearn making myself small and instead learn I had a right to take up space, to feel things, and to be loved by others, and most importantly by me. I now run because I enjoy it, I stick with running plans and am careful to not overdo it. I also have worked with a dietitian, and those things along with the critically important emotional healing, I have created a healthy relationship with food and exercise.

We can overcome difficult things and change our way of thinking. Again, the power comes through processing the emotions. When we change our feelings, we can change our thoughts, mindset, and behaviors.

I didn't just decide to starve myself and overexercise, I had powerful emotions I didn't have an outlet for, and the more they crowded in on me, the more I tried to numb them.

In my healing practice and working with clients one-on-one, I started to see a similar pattern in each and every person. In some people, it was more pronounced than in others, but it all came back to the same core issue. While each person was experiencing different things, the underlying current driving all of the pain and suffering pointed directly back to not feeling good enough, and to not having a healthy amount of self-love.

Self-love can be a tricky thing. Even when we become good at loving who we are, it can still be easy to fall back into old patterns and beliefs when we forget we deserve love too. Our inclination when things are difficult is so often to stop providing ourselves love and give less and less to our own heart, when in fact, these are the times we need to redouble our efforts and give more and more love to ourselves.

Self-love can also be hard sometimes because many of us believe loving who we are is wrong. One Sunday morning at church, I slipped out to use the restroom, and when I went to open the bathroom door, a little girl jumped away and looked quite embarrassed to see me. I saw she was holding a crown in her hand as I walked past and apologized for scaring her when I opened the door. I didn't think much of the crown until I walked out of the stall and went to the sink to wash my hands. I saw on the counter there were some decorations, including two small crowns. I suddenly realized the little girl had been trying to see herself in the mirror wearing one of the crowns. I smiled and wished she was still there, I would have told her how beautiful she looked in it, and I hope that is what she saw when she checked out her reflection. We deserve the goodness that comes from seeing our own beauty within, and we need to believe we are worthy of love.

So, what exactly is self-love? Part of self-love is having a healthy respect for our own needs, own happiness, and own choices. It's also about taking care of those things without sacrificing yourself to make others happy. It's about being authentic and true to who you really are. Self-love is quiet. It's between you and you alone. It's not boastful, bragging, or looking for validation from outside of yourself. On the contrary, it is exactly opposite of that. Instead of looking for outside validation, it seeks to find approval from within oneself.

There are people who seem to "love" themselves in a way that feels very unloving. The word "seems" in that sentence is the important word because it's not love at all. It's something different all together. It's a form of insecurity and self-doubt that relies on other people to validate their worth. It's not love, it's conceit, sometimes narcissism, and it is looking outward for what can only be found inward. Those things are manipulative and come from a place of scarcity and fear.

Self-love is gentle, and it's healthy, we all need it, and the more the better. When we are loving ourselves by being kind, understanding, and accepting of who we are, it is far easier to do the same for others. The little girl with the crown is a perfect example of the quietness of self-love. She was having a moment with herself, admiring her own beauty and potential.

Are self-love and self-esteem the same thing? No, while they go hand in hand, they do differ. Self-esteem is feeling good and proud about yourself in non-arrogant ways, but self-love is more of an acceptance of who you are, flaws and all; because we ALL have them. This unconditional acceptance is what helps you to want to take care of yourself, to speak kindly to yourself, and to focus on what makes you happy. Self-love is a feeling, but it's also a choice and an action.

Have you ever had a plant that just seemed to not want to grow, or that was turning brown and dropping leaves? I have. I have this plant that was actually given to my son, but he asked me to take care of it because his apartment didn't have any sunny windows. It seemed to do ok at first, but over time started losing leaves and looking very sad. I kept limping it along, but admittedly didn't go above and beyond for it.

One day I decided to do something active to try and improve it. I gave it a bigger container and new soil. I started noticing it pepping up. That encouraged me to pay more attention to it, as I was marveling at its growth and how nice it looked. Soon it was growing bigger and looked greener than ever. While a plant isn't terribly high maintenance, it does require adequate water and sunlight, a nice pot, and some dirt. I received this plant in a small pot and just expected it to do well without offering it much more than occasional water and wondered why it didn't look better.

I was giving it the bare minimum. I think we tend to do that to ourselves too. We rush around and give to others all day and leave very little time for what we ourselves need. This is often seen as some kind of badge of honor. But when we give of ourselves until we are depleted, we struggle to grow or appreciate our own beautiful qualities, and we begin to wither away just like the leaves on my plant did. Notice how I was surprised at the growth of the plant when I began to give it some attention and felt encouraged to do just a bit more? I think a self-love practice works that way too. When we start making changes and then see some results, it makes us want more.

There's a children's book called *The Giving Tree* by Shel Silverstein. You've probably read it at one time or another. In that book, a little boy loves a tree, and the tree loves him. The tree loves the boy so much in fact, she is willing to give all she has for his happiness. The tree offers a trunk for climbing, branches for swinging, leaves for shade, and apples to eat. She gives and gives and is happy…or so she says. All the while the tree is saying she is happy, but the story feels so sad. The more she gives, the demands on the tree become greater, she not only gives some apples, she gives all of her apples to the boy to sell, then she gives her branches for him to build a house, and last her trunk for the boy to make a boat. Eventually, the tree has nothing left to give. While it is wonderful to help others and to give love freely and without condition, we must remember to not give every scrap of ourselves away, or like the tree, we will be reduced to nothing more than an old stump. I've always liked this book, even though it is sad, because it is also a good lesson to remember we need to nourish ourselves and even say no sometimes to be able to give ourselves love too.

We strive to love others unconditionally, but how about how we love ourselves? Do we put conditions on accepting who we are? Does our self-confidence drop when we've not been as successful as we'd hoped with something? Are we telling ourselves we are worthy "if" or "when" we can do something that proves we have value? If you find yourself doing these things, ask yourself, "Would I treat another this way?" Would I put if/then statements on my relationship with my best friend, my spouse, my child, my mother? Of course, you wouldn't. You wouldn't tell your partner you only love them if they do something amazing at work, or if they lose ten pounds, right?

So why do we do that to ourselves?

When we do not love the person we are, everything in life becomes more difficult. We struggle with decisions, self-doubt, unworthiness, feeling stuck, having poor communication with others, codependency, addictions, and other destructive behaviors and the list goes on. A practice of self-love is critical to our happiness, health, and well-being. Try to say something kind and loving to yourself each and every day, and many times a day at that.

When I was in college studying photography, I was scheduled to have a show of my work at the library. This was kind of a big deal, and I was really excited to get my photographs mounted and hung. It was a lot of work preparing all of the images, and a lot of money for a college student. I finally got them displayed, and I put an empty book with a pen out for people to make comments. When the show was over a few weeks later, I sat down and looked through the book. There was beautiful comment after beautiful comment. And then... one negative comment. It said, "Looks like work from a happy snappy." Almost thirty years later, I don't remember the positive comments, but I do remember that negative one. Why is that? What makes it so easy to accept criticism but not praise?

This happens because of something called the negativity bias. We are more apt to pay attention to negative comments before we will receive praise. The negative statements stay with us far longer as well. Case in point, my photography show book. Those words burned in my brain and remain today. While the comment wasn't even that harsh, it hurt because I was working hard at being a professional, and I felt reduced to a snap happy picture taker. My mind translated this to not being serious, and my work was mediocre at best.

There was something inside me that took the negative comment and created this greater story about myself. If I had more confidence and healthy self-worth, I would have likely just laughed it off and said, "Out of all of these pages of comments, there's going to be at least one that isn't favorable."

When we work on our feeling of worth with a self-love practice, we can change our brain to be able to more readily appreciate and accept praise and be less likely to grab onto the negative statements made about us. It's sort of like putting a shield around yourself so that the negativity bounces off.

You can create your shield by cultivating a self-love practice, and most importantly, by being consistent with it. It's not a one hour or one day thing, it needs to become a part of your every day, even if it's just catching yourself in a moment where you are not being loving toward yourself and turning it around.

Another way to increase self-love is to practice self-care. Self-care isn't about being indulgent and selfish. It's about taking care of your body, your mind, and your spirit. So that you are able to do your job, take care of your family, and any other responsibilities or commitments you may have. This can be accomplished in many ways.

Here are a few:

- Get a massage
- Get adequate sleep
- Provide good nutrition for yourself
- Exercise (don't over exercise though, that ends up going the opposite direction)
- Love your body…every part of it, unconditionally
- Don't compare yourself to others or worry about what others think. There is only one you
- Spend time in nature
- Meditate or pray
- Take a nap
- Journal
- Read a book
- Say no to something
- Call a friend

KEY FOR CHANGE

Self-love exercises to start today:

Questions to consider: What in your life is a way you are being unkind and unloving toward yourself?

Are you berating yourself about your parenting skills? About your job? About your accomplishments?

Ask yourself (and be honest!) How do I feel about me?

It might be time to really look at whether or not you love and accept who you are, and what feelings and/or past situations are holding you back from providing loving acceptance of yourself.

Are you providing adequate self-care in your daily routine? In what way could you change that if the answer is no?

If the answer is yes, good job, keep doing it!

If it helps, get yourself a crown and do a little reflection check in from time to time and remember you are good and worthy. As a bonus, this will help you connect to your inner child.

I'm Possible

Have you ever noticed how fast a weed grows?

Anyone who is interested in gardening knows we spend tons of time perfecting beautiful landscapes. We invest a great deal of time and care into growing perfect, healthy flowers, yet a weed will sprout and grow massive, seemingly overnight. How is it the beautiful things take time and care, yet the thorny, ugly nuisances with deep and strong roots appear without any direct focus on them?

Emotional "weeds" grow with the same fervor when we speak negatively to ourselves and when we forget to practice self-care. What if we cultivated our emotional health with care and concern like we do our flower beds and vegetable gardens? What if we fed our own being with loving, kind, and grace-filled thoughts and words? If we take time to nurture a healthy garden with our emotions, we will grow beautiful and strong. The roots of the weeds will shrivel and die, and the roses from our soul will thrive and bloom.

Research shows in a typical day, the average person has 60,000 thoughts, and about 80 percent of those are negative. Shockingly, around 90 percent of the thoughts we have in a day get repeated the next day. So, in essence, we are living in the same loop of negative thoughts over and over. It's no wonder it's difficult to break a negative thought cycle. The more we do something, the more it becomes habit, and so if day after day, year after year, we are reinforcing the exact same negative thoughts, it would be difficult to change. But it's not impossible. To quote my all-time favorite actress, Audrey Hepburn, "Nothing is impossible, the word itself says 'I'm possible!'"

How true is that? "I'm possible." Yes, I am possible, and it is possible to be however we wish to be. This is everyone's reality. We all have a deep well of possibility within us, and the more we reach into that well, the more we bring to the surface. Our thirst for knowing ourselves is quenched when we face the hard stuff, and when we believe deeply in our own possibility.

Self-talk is the narrative you have inside your head. The way we talk in our own mind matters greatly toward our mental health and general outlook on life. Self-talk can be positive or negative. Negative self-talk contributes to lack of confidence, low self-worth, and a generally bad view of oneself and the world. This negative talk can make us feel stuck, lost, anxious, depressed, and uncertain about what we want or need. Conversely, positive self-talk can build confidence, self-worth, and have a big impact on our ability to succeed, and be happy and healthy. Positive self-talk can help you feel more in control of your life, like things are not happening to you, but rather *for* you.

Paying attention to which one you naturally gravitate toward is a key element in changing patterns and beliefs. If you are constantly reinforcing a negatively held belief about yourself, you will stay stuck in an endless loop of the same behaviors you participate in, even if they are bad for you. If you constantly talk negatively to yourself, judge yourself, criticize, or call yourself names, eventually, you will begin to believe all of those things on a deeper level, *even though they are not true*.

The good news is this can be changed! We can train our brains to think differently. You are the only one in control of your thoughts, therefore, you can decide what ideas about yourself reside in your mind. If you want happiness, good health, and positive self-worth, begin to change the things you say to yourself in your head. When you've processed your negative feelings, this makes room to create positive thoughts.

What is the voice in your head saying most often? Take a moment and really think about this. Also, notice, do you ever speak negatively about yourself in a joking way? I suspect this is a yes for nearly everyone. Who hasn't said "Oh, I'm so stupid, I did this (insert whatever) again!" I know I have, though since I've learned our subconscious mind doesn't understand a joke versus truth, and only understands the words we speak in quite a literal way, I have worked hard at silencing those "jokes," and I hope you will too.

When we react to someone in a way that makes them feel criticized, they are not likely to want to bend our way and cooperate, right?

I think this applies to ourselves as well. When we are constantly critical of ourself, our subconscious or inner being is not so willing to work with us.

If you provide loving interactions with yourself, you will find it easier over time to get to the place you want to be. Imagine talking to yourself as if you were talking to your best friend. If you find you are saying something to yourself there is no way you would say to a friend, or to a child, then stop yourself in the moment and turn it around.

This is a good litmus test. If you know for a fact you would never utter the words you spoke or thought to your best friend or an innocent child, you will know, too, you should not say them to yourself. You deserve the same loving care you give others. You are worthy of that.

The greatest number of conversations you will ever have will be with yourself. Make them kind, loving, forgiving, and uplifting. Again, there is a difference between narcissism and speaking positively to oneself. The kindness we provide ourselves in our own minds comes out in many positive ways to affect others as well. When we feel good about ourselves, the energy we put out into the world is positive too, and that can help others see the goodness in themselves. Can you think of someone you genuinely enjoy being around because they exude positivity and seem to almost glow from within? If so, they are likely speaking positively to themselves, and that energy shines as if they had a newly charged battery in them. We have the power to charge our battery by providing loving reminders to ourself we are worthy of goodness. Others will see that light coming from us like a beacon calling to them, and they will want the same.

Are there things you say repeatedly to yourself that perpetuate a bad habit or behavior you dislike or want to change? For example, do you choose to eat things that are bad for you, but you tell yourself you are addicted and can't stop? By saying those words, you tell your brain it might as well eat what you are not supposed to, because you have no power over it. But that's a lie, you DO have power over what you eat. Sure, you may prefer a bowl of ice cream to a salad, but you do have the choice in which of those you partake in. If you instead change the words you say to yourself to be something like "I can decide what I want to eat, and no food controls my mind or choices," you will have better results.

The same would apply to a goal. If you were trying to accomplish something but continually tell yourself you just can't get it done, it will inevitably be true. We must change the narrative we speak in order to get the results we want. Try it. Think of something you are struggling with, whether it's a behavior or something you want to achieve. Now, think about the primary messages you give yourself about that particular thing. Are they positive or negative? Writing this down so you can see it will help too.

Here's an example:

If you want to lose twenty pounds, but it's not happening, think about the message you give yourself. Is it something like: "I can't lose weight, it's too hard, and I hate exercise."

Every time you tell yourself you hate exercise, your mind agrees and stops you from wanting to do it. You'll always find something else to do instead because you are instructing your brain to do just that.

Now, write down what a new narrative could be.

Maybe something like: "I will lose twenty pounds, I enjoy exercise, it's good for my health, and I'm worth it."

Say this to yourself as often as possible and watch how your behavior changes. You are giving your subconscious mind a new belief and new instructions to carry out which will create the change you desire.

KEY FOR CHANGE

If you find yourself frequently speaking negatively to yourself, try this: Sometime when you are feeling really good about yourself, and your self-worth is in a good place, or if this doesn't seem to happen for you, take a moment and imagine what it would feel like to have really high self-worth. Imagine the feeling of confidence and love for yourself. What do you want to feel like? Now, with that really good feeling in mind, think of a positive image. Maybe it's a sunrise that makes you feel like love and hope, or a majestic tree that emanates peace and strength. Now, pair the feeling and the image and use it as a sort of "touchstone" to return to when you find yourself in a loop of negativity. Practice this often, and it will become your go-to response when you are not speaking kindly to yourself. It will serve as a reminder of what you really want to feel, and then you can use that to help you flip your thoughts from the negative to the positive.

Some positive Self-Talk Statements to start using now:

* I am enough.

* My challenges help me grow.

* Today is going to be my day.

* I can make a difference.

* I am an original.

* I am building my future.

* I can do this!

* I am working on myself.

* I am allowed to learn.

* I am powerful.

* I have so much to be proud of.

* I trust myself to succeed.

* I am calm and confident.

* I am taking things one step at a time.

* I am moving toward my goals.

Can you name some others?

Find a few you like or that support a particular goal you have and write them someplace you will see them throughout your day. Maybe on a sticky note on your mirror, or your computer monitor. Repeating positive self-talk statements often will help you believe in yourself and create a greater sense of self-love and self-worth which are building blocks to just about everything. When we feel good about ourselves, everything becomes easier.

PART II

Mindset changes that can come from emotional processing

When we learn how to feel our feelings, we can begin to change our thoughts, habits, patterns and beliefs.

In the first part of the book, we learned the importance of connecting to our subconscious mind to access our true feelings and beliefs. Once we process those feelings and challenge the beliefs we may have held that haven't worked for us, we can choose to make powerful and lasting changes in our life by examining and challenging our mindsets.

What are mindsets anyway?

A mindset is the set of beliefs we have that shape our view of ourself and the world around us. The reason emotional processing is important to creating powerful mindset shifts is because we can't change what we think unless we confront and dive into what we feel. When we work through our feelings, we can come to a place of clarity. When we have clarity, we can look at our mindset with fresh eyes, and instead of going along with what we've always done, we can begin to do what truly feels right for us.

There are many different kinds of mindsets. We can go from fixed to growth, scarcity to abundance. We can leave behind behaviors like having poor boundaries, living in fear, perfectionism, victimhood, limiting beliefs, and more. Our mind can change about any of these things when we acknowledge and process any negative emotions that are keeping us stuck in ways of thinking that are not positive or helpful to us.

CHAPTER 10

CASE CLOSED

Through judging we separate,
through understanding we grow

~Doe Zantamata, *TheMindsJournal*

Have you ever met someone and instantly decided you knew something about them just based on your initial impression? Have you ever been wrong about that once you got to know them?

Before we can really know someone, we have to learn to understand them. This applies to ourselves as well. In order to really know who we are and what we desire, we must go on a self-reflective journey and sort through our feelings about our experiences. As we follow the process, we will find we are judging ourselves less and less, because we are understanding ourselves more and more. Too often, though, we are stuck in a loop of judgment about what we've done wrong and struggle to see what we've done right. This contributes to feelings of unworthiness.

If we believe we are not worthy, that story will continue to play out for us again and again. I'm showing my age here, but if you remember record players, you will recall sometimes the needle would get stuck, and the song at first might seem like it's going to play, but then it skips and plays the same line again, over and over. The only way to fix this, was to pick the needle up and start it again. If you find yourself in a loop of judgment of yourself or someone else, pause, evaluate what you are doing, thinking, or saying, and start again. You are allowed to learn. We can learn acceptance through recognizing we are all human, and we all have our own unique challenges.

When we are judging others, we may want to consider how we are judging ourselves as well. Judgment is something we tend to do quickly, based on very little and often surface level information. Many years ago, after moving to a new town, where I knew only a few people, I joined a gym and spent many months, maybe even a year, being a total loner, working out and running solo. It was a hard time in my life, and I was dealing with depression and loneliness. One day, a beautiful blonde woman who looked to be about my age approached me on the track and with the sweetest southern accent introduced herself and said, "We need you in our running group." I was so surprised to be approached after finding it so hard to break into any social circle since moving there from a bigger city. I am an introvert by nature, but at that time was also quite shy, and by the way, they are not the same thing as I came to learn. Introverts enjoy time alone and can get drained being around too many people, but people who are shy are actually afraid to interact with others, though don't necessarily want to be alone. I learned to later embrace my introversion and challenge my shyness.

I started running with this lovely lady and getting to know her, and we became great friends. She introduced me to others, as well as sharing with me, she had noticed me alone for quite a while and wondered if I, like her, had moved from somewhere else. She was a fitness instructor and Zumba dance teacher and invited me to her classes. I had never done Zumba before and felt very out of my element but was willing to try.

After a few classes, I started noticing a couple girls in the front row who were Zumba naturals seemed to be whispering about me. Of course, sometimes we think someone is talking about us, when they are not. However, I learned they were in fact talking about me, as one of them had approached my new friend and told her I seemed like a real "snob," and I "thought I was better than them because I never talked to them."

Wow.

I was stunned.

I never talked to them because I was intimidated by how well they seemed to know and pick up the dances while I was stumbling over my feet and trying not to look ridiculous. I had made a judgment about these ladies with perfect dance skills thinking they would never want to talk to me, and at the same time, they had made a judgment based on my silence. We were not understanding each other at all.

When I heard they thought I was a snob, I was hurt to say the least. My friend corrected them and said, "She's not a snob, she's shy."

Here was a perfect example of how people take very limited superficial information based only on what was observed and created a judgment.

They said I was a "snob" because I didn't talk to them. Likewise, I didn't talk to them because I thought they were superior to me and obviously wouldn't want to spend time with me. This was a classic case of judgment of others, and we were probably all judging ourselves a bit in this too. We were driven by fear and lack of information. The human tendency to create a story to make ourselves feel better is all too common.

Recently on Facebook, I saw a picture of a celebrity clearly wearing makeup, but the article headline said this person posted a selfie on their fiftieth birthday with no makeup and no filters. As I was approaching my own fiftieth, I immediately was drawn to the story and her appearance. Before opening the article, I decided to scroll through the comments. Not surprisingly, so many of them said "She clearly has makeup on!" Outraged lines of "What a lie!" showed up in comment after comment. The majority of the comments were from women. I then went and opened the article, and sure enough, there was a photo of the celebrity on her fiftieth birthday with no makeup, no filters, hair undone, and looking very relaxed in sweatpants in her home.

I thought this was an interesting statement about judgment, and how often people judge others without any real information about them. Why is this our first inclination? If people had taken a moment to open the article, they would have seen the real picture and recognized the fact she was being honest. I'm sure the writer of the story was after the result they got, with people making comments to increase their views, and it didn't matter it was a misrepresentation of the celebrity with the headline photo chosen. The people making comments made a judgment based on a few words they saw in the headline of the article. Why do we do this? Women especially, why would we knock another woman down like this? How often are we judging without having all of the information?

We cannot accept and love others with open arms if we are approaching ourselves with criticism and punishment. If we can release judgment of ourselves, we will find judgment of others naturally falls away, and again, this will come through understanding who we are and really acknowledging our feelings and experiences. We are all equally worthy and all doing the best we can with where we are at that given time. Doing our best will change from day to day, sometimes hour to hour. We do the best with what we have emotionally, spiritually, financially, energetically, etc. Some days we have more, some days we have less, but if we are using the knowledge, compassion, understanding, and resources we have in that given moment, it is the best we can do.

This is where grace comes in. We must allow grace for the things that are in flux, for the things that change sometimes without our ability to control. If we can give ourselves grace in our mistakes and know we have done our best, we can offer the same to others. Just imagine for a moment you are them and look at more than surface level information. If you don't have more than surface level information, close your eyes and imagine what it must feel like to be that new person in the room who knows no one, who doesn't know the dance steps, who is already shy, feeling depressed, and maybe a little lost. You'll be able to see something on a soul level that provides some understanding maybe you don't know their story, but there's always more to the story, and we must allow grace for the pieces we don't know. So, in this example, maybe you only know they are new in town. The rest you will get when you pause and recognize that no, you don't know their story, but there's likely much more to it than what you see at first glance.

We won't always get things right, but we can always try again. The kindlier we can approach ourselves, the kindlier we will approach others. When we seem to be at our worst, that is when we need grace, love, and acceptance the most.

If you ever find yourself talking badly about someone else, stop for a moment and ask yourself is this something I believe about me? Or do I somehow feel I'm better than this person and therefore want to diminish them a little? If we begin to pick up on things that bother us in other people— maybe the way they do something, maybe the way they talk about someone—if we really truly look inward and examine ourselves, it's very likely we will see we are in fact behaving the very way we claim to despise. When we can see our own faults and begin to accept ourselves in spite of them, we will be less likely to call them out in others. As with so many things, it all begins with you.

Sometimes of course, what we see in someone else doesn't match a behavior or quality we have, and in those cases, it's still important to offer grace and kindness because we do not know why they are behaving the way they are. It is not up to us to cast judgment. After all, we may do something someone else wouldn't, and wouldn't we like to have that compassion as well?

Sending blessings to people rather than feeling negative toward them can completely change the energy of the situation. Love carries healing energy. Don't be confused by what I mean by love. Yes, love can be an intimate relationship with a lover, but also a relationship with a friend, parent, child, or even a stranger. Love is the energy we must strive to put out into the world. If you are struggling with someone, start sending them "blessings" for what they might need most, just as I described in the chapter on forgiveness. Maybe they need self-worth, kindness, or peace. I know it sounds crazy, but it really has the power to shift the energy of a situation.

A few years ago, some friends and I were coming back from running a race out of town and my friend was driving. As she went to merge onto a busy road, a car that was in front of her braked, but she had already begun the merge. She lightly tapped his bumper, and it was quickly evident the man was enraged. He pulled into the parking lot of a nearby bank and got out yelling at my friend. He examined his car, to which there was no visible damage, and continued to berate her. He wanted to exchange information "just in case." It was completely absurd. I stood outside the car with them as my friend was writing down her info, and as I waited, I began sending the man blessings.

You might ask how or why I would do that to someone who was so angry with my friend, but I knew the energy of those thoughts could possibly make things better. I was sending him blessings for understanding, for kindness and clear vision rather than judging his anger and criticism. Before they were done with the information exchange, something happened with the man. He suddenly shifted. He decided he didn't in fact need her info, his car was clearly not damaged, and we could just go on our way. My friend and I got back in her car, and she turned to me, stunned, and asked, "What just happened here?" I said, "I don't know, but I would like to think the man felt the energy of love." We decided we didn't know for sure, but it certainly didn't hurt, because in any case, if you are not responding in anger, the other will feel it on some level, and if nothing else, you won't subject yourself to angry thoughts that won't change anything. I've been reminded of that in many other tense situations and have noticed when I can step back and just focus on putting the energy of love out, things are so much easier. Try it the next time you are experiencing a challenge with someone, or if you feel you are judging or being judged by someone. Ask yourself what does the other person need right now in order to be more loving and accepting and then say those words either in your mind or out loud if appropriate. In the case of my example, I said in my mind, "May you be blessed with understanding, kindness, and clear vision." It can never hurt to put loving energy out into the world. It will always contribute to less judgment even just within yourself.

 **KEY FOR CHANGE**

Exercises to end judgment

Focus on the positives about yourself and look for positives in others. Again, if we can find the good, we are not creating judgments.

Consider this: What if we are all doing the best we can with where we currently are on our journey...including YOU?

Accept compliments with gratitude.

So often we struggle to accept compliments because we are in judgment of ourselves. Try just saying thank you next time someone offers you praise.

Exercise:

Fold a piece of paper in half, and on one side write down a judgment or criticism you have of yourself, then on the other side, write a self-compassionate response to the criticism. Step back and imagine you are writing a response to a friend or family member if that makes it easier at first. You deserve the same compassion you would so easily give someone else.

CHAPTER 11

It's Ok to Push Back

*When you say 'yes' to others,
make sure you are not saying 'no' to yourself.*

~Paulo Coelho, *Facebook, April 11, 2020*

Let's talk a bit about boundaries. First of all, what is a boundary? If a boundary on a map shows where one state or country ends and another begins, an energetic or personal boundary shows where I end and you begin and vice versa. Each state or country has its own set of rules and culture, and each person does too. Think of where the property lines around your house are. They are invisible lines, but your neighbors on each side are aware of where those lines are, as are you. We don't need fences or walls to respect those property lines. (Most of the time anyway!) We wouldn't go into our neighbor's yard and pick apples from their tree or flowers from their garden without consent, and likewise, we shouldn't invade someone else's personal energy, time, or physical boundaries. We have invisible lines that separate us from all others as well. Those lines are what we will accept in a relationship. They are what keep us feeling like we are in control of our own lives.

It's very important to have good boundaries with others, or else we will find ourselves being taken advantage of, ordered around, and generally disrespected. Boundaries are healthy and necessary. We teach others how to treat us. If we have poor boundaries, we are letting people know they can control us. If we don't create our own boundaries, we also may not recognize the boundaries of others and may disrespect someone without it being our intention.

I spoke at a women's conference recently, and there was a self-defense demonstration by the lunch keynote speaker, Gloria Marcott, founder of Soul Punch Power Academy for Women who aspires to train one million women to know how to protect themselves. While she focuses on physical protection, she also unknowingly taught a lesson in emotional safety. She had two women stand about fifteen feet apart. She then told one woman when the other got too close, she was to put her hand up to stop her. She instructed the other woman to run at the first woman with full speed. It was interesting to watch. At first, the woman putting her hand up stopped her about five feet away. After repeating several times, the second woman got closer and closer. It was like the first woman got used to her pushing in on her boundary and gave in a bit.

I wonder how often we do this with our emotional boundaries too. Do we create boundaries and then get relaxed about them and subsequently wonder why things feel wrong with certain people? Have we stopped holding our boundary to "be nice" or "keep the peace"? Is that hurting us in the process? What about with this physical demonstration. If the first woman just stopped putting her hand up, she would have taken the full blow from the second woman and been knocked down. Even though she allowed her to get closer, she never totally gave up the boundary. If we wouldn't do this when protecting our physical body, why do we allow our boundaries to be pushed emotionally and energetically past what is comfortable to us?

I used to really struggle with boundaries because of a deep desire to make everyone happy all the time. It's still a place where I'm a work in progress, but I'm miles better than I used to be. If we have weak or non-existent boundaries, we may end up feeling disrespected and controlled, drained and almost dreading contact with the person or persons we are lacking those boundaries with. We might find ourselves angry with that person for continuing to take advantage of us, when in reality we do have control over that. If we have a drink and hand it to someone, we can't be angry with them for draining the glass if we are the one that gave them the straw.

In order to set boundaries in relationships, we must decide what is good for us and what we want. By having a mature conversation rather than avoiding talking about what is bothering us, we can create mutual respect and prevent resentment from building. When we allow what we are not ok with in order to please others or avoid conflict, we actually create conflict, but within ourselves. It's important to maintain a balance in all personal connections. Boundaries are necessary with romantic partners, friends, family members, coworkers, and yes, even strangers.

Creating healthy boundaries for ourselves is a form of

self-care and goes a very long way toward helping us feel empowered and in control of our own life. A few years ago, I had a situation with someone where I had a lack of boundaries, and it started to take a toll on my mental health and well-being, and over time, my physical health too. The person was a bit emotionally fragile, and so when they started asking more things of me, I complied because I reasoned they were hurting from their own traumas, and I thought maybe I could help them. At first, it wasn't bad. I enjoyed their company, and the relationship felt pretty balanced. As time went on, I began to feel taken advantage of and manipulated. Remember that physical boundary demonstration? I essentially stopped putting my hand up and allowed them to get closer and closer even though it made me uncomfortable.

Other friends would remark I looked like my joy was draining away when they saw me. They didn't even know what was really going on with this other person. I kept trying to help, comfort, and support them, but the demands got bigger and bigger, and I started to feel like they owned me. They wanted me to talk on the phone at least once a week, and the calls would go on for hours. I spoke very little on the calls, they were just dumping all of their stress and drama on me. I started to feel like they were running my life, but in essence, they were ruining it. It started creating problems with my family as this person was always seeking my attention and showing up at my house, not respecting my work schedule or other commitments. I began to feel anxious and dread whenever I knew an interaction with them was coming. It went on for over a year until I felt like I couldn't take it anymore.

I consulted a therapist to try and figure out what I could do to repair this. In the end, I had to create a somewhat extreme boundary by letting the person know I couldn't have them in my life at all anymore, and then I subsequently blocked them on my phone and social media.

Almost instantly, I felt better. It was almost as if I had been holding my breath and now, I could finally exhale. The relief was palpable. Others noticed a new revived lightness to me. I was no longer having anxiety every time my phone buzzed with a text. It was a necessary boundary. I took control of my own life, I was assertive, and I finally said what I needed and followed through. If I'd had better boundaries at the outset, it wouldn't have had to get to the point of making myself physically ill, emotionally strained, and off balance in the first place.

So, how do you know if you need a boundary with someone? Well, for starters, pay attention to how your body feels when you are around them. If you notice tension in your neck, throat, or shoulders, an uneasy stomach, pounding in your head, or anxiousness growing only when you get a text from them, know you'll be seeing them, or have to talk to them, it's a pretty good sign you need a boundary. Also notice if the relationship is one-sided. By that I mean are you always doing things for them, or what they want without any reciprocation from them? If so, you probably need a boundary. Some of the best advice I've gotten about dealing with people is to "match their effort." If you are the one always making an effort to please someone or accommodate them, and they are taking from you and not offering true care or support in return, that is once again a sign a boundary needs to be made.

It's taken me a good bit of practice to step back and observe my interactions with people to assess what the relationship actually is. If I feel used and manipulated, I make note of it. If I feel like it's work to try and interact with someone, I tend to pull back. If I notice any time spent with the person leaves me feeling drained, I know it's time to change the relationship. It is not wrong to take care of your needs too. We are not required to be friends with, date, or even keep family members who are toxic in our circle. We are allowed to choose who we give our energy to. This becomes much easier when we work through the emotions that have had us unable to create healthy boundaries previously. It may be because we are struggling with self-worth and are used to being "people pleasers," or it may be because we are looking for validation and acceptance and think if we say no, we are somehow unlovable.

Boundaries are not a bad thing, and if someone perceives them as such, then it's definitely a sign a boundary was needed. No one has the right to control what you do, how you spend your time, what you think, or say. If someone is not taking your feelings into consideration, then a boundary is most certainly needed. Decide what it is that works for you with that person and carry it through. If that means having a difficult conversation, remember once you do it, you will reap the reward of greater peace.

So, what does a boundary look like? Well, it might be not responding immediately to a text, or taking your time to return a phone call. Maybe it's saying you prefer a different activity to what you are being asked to do. It might be asking someone to respect your time, your space, and your wishes. It might be not doing something you don't want to. It's perfectly ok to say no. Sometimes a boundary is simply the word "no" with no further explanation. Having a boundary means you take responsibility for your own actions, but not the actions of others. We are all responsible for our own emotions and what we do or say. You are more likely to set good and appropriate boundaries if you have strong self-esteem. When our self-esteem is low, so, too, are our boundaries. We will allow too much and take too much responsibility for others. The good news is both of these things can be changed and improved. If you respect yourself, you will be willing to ask others to do so as well.

KEY FOR CHANGE

Recognize where you have good boundaries and where your boundaries might need a little improvement.

Is there a person that makes you feel uncomfortable, stressed, unappreciated, or overwhelmed?

Determine what you need to feel like you have a good boundary with that person.

What makes you feel safe, comfortable, seen, heard, and respected?

What is currently happening with that person, and is it in alignment with what you need? If it's not in alignment, what changes can you make to get it there?

Visualize your boundary. Come up with a plan to execute it.

It may look like this: "When you talk to me that way, it makes me feel _____, and I'm asking you to stop please. If you don't respect my needs, then I will have to stop spending time with you."

Stand firm in what you have decided and create the boundary with the confidence you are worth it, you deserve to have physical, energetic, and emotional boundaries that are in alignment with your needs.

CHAPTER 12

CHANGE THE CHANNEL

You are the master of your destiny. You can influence, direct and control your own environment. You can make your life what you want it to be.

~Napoleon Hill, *Think and Grow Rich*

Do you feel like you are in control of your life, or like you are bouncing here and there just letting whatever happens happen? Or worse still, are you letting others tell you what to do, what to feel, how to be? Maybe you are trying to squeeze yourself into an image someone else has for you. Maybe you are trying to meet expectations you can't possibly even reach. Maybe you even sabotage your own plans by not having faith in your abilities or ideas.

If you want something to be different, then you can't sit around waiting for it to show up. When we do the same things day after day, each day that arrives will be a repeat of the previous one in some way. You are in the driver's seat of your life, and the destinations are endless. Make a choice to create your own map and go where you feel you belong, not where anyone else tells you that you do.

Sometimes we have to turn down many different roads before we find the one that fits us best, the one with the scenery that makes us feel at peace, and the path that leads us closer to our true destination. If we start down one route and we get an uneasy feeling, we can easily readjust. The problems happen when we ignore the unsettled feeling and just keep driving.

Speaking of cars, one day recently, I was driving down the road, and a song came on the radio I don't particularly care for, and I was immediately thinking "Ugh, I don't like this song, I can't wait until it's over." I continued driving while listening to the song I dislike, and all of a sudden, I was struck with how funny that was. I had the power to change the song mere inches away from me. All I had to do was push a button, and I had other choices quite literally at my fingertips! Life is truly this way too. If we don't like a situation we are in or something is not going well, we have the power and the choice to make a conscious change. So often, though, we stay stuck because somewhere inside ourselves we believe change is beyond our reach.

Of course, there will be things in life we can't completely change, like if someone leaves our life by their choice or by death, we can't make them come back. For those instances, we need to process and accept our feelings until we can find peace, but for the most part, we can make changes to situations that are not what we envision or want for our lives. I'm not saying it's easy, but anything is possible if we are willing to face the challenging things. This may mean difficult conversations, hard work, a lot of uncomfortableness, and other somewhat (or completely) painful actions, realizations, and acceptance.

But if we truly want something different, we can reach out and change the radio station and find the song that speaks to us and fulfills our dreams.

One evening in the summer, I noticed there were seven frogs in our pool. I knew the chlorine was not good for them, and they really needed to get out. I started trying to scoop them out with the net. I'd get one out, then while I was working on rescuing the next one, the first one would jump back in. This went on for a little while until I realized they were not on board with my efforts to save them.

How often do we do this to ourselves? We start to find a place where we begin to make changes, but something inside of us says this is uncomfortable, so I'm just going to go back to what I already know, even though it is hurting me? This is a way we sabotage our dreams and goals.

In the case of my amphibious friends, they were uneasy being scooped from the comfort of water and being plopped onto concrete next to a human, and so even though the water they were pulled from was not good for them, they went back to it because they were uncomfortable in the new situation.

Oftentimes, we sabotage ourselves because it starts feeling uncomfortable when we begin moving past the highest level of success or happiness we have ever felt. In those moments, we have the choice to move toward new heights or stay where we are. Fear is usually the reason we stay in one place.

This pattern can be changed when we acknowledge that

fear and ask ourselves what we are truly afraid of. Usually, we have told ourselves a story of "what could happen" that is rarely true. Feel the fear, challenge the fear, and then it's possible to break through it.

We tend to stay stuck in a situation or a belief because our subconscious just likes that "cozy, I know what to expect" feeling...even when it's more like a kick in the gut than an enveloping hug. What I'm trying to say is situations and behaviors can be comfortable while being completely uncomfortable. What's that saying? Two things can be true at the same time. Yes, this is an instance like that. It can be true what you currently know is comfortable because you are already conditioned to create the responses that keep things peaceful, or don't make waves, or just are at a level of hard you already know how to manage. All the while it can still be true this very same situation is excruciatingly painful because you know it's wrong for you.

Imagine you are standing in front of a row of doors. Through each door is an option for your life. Now, what if you always walk through the third door. You walk through it day after day, never even looking at the other doors. Or maybe, you take a quick glance at the other choices, but still take the steps through the third door. What if, as you do this, you also realize what you experience through that third door is terribly uncomfortable for you. What if it really is creating angst in your life? Could it be a job that is overly stressful and unfulfilling? Are you in an unhealthy relationship? Is a toxic friend slowly poisoning you? Are you looking wistfully at dreams you have without taking steps to make them happen?

You have all these other doors, but when you go through the third door, you know what is going to happen, so you keep walking in. You show up day after day at the job you hate, you argue constantly with your partner, you get pushed around by a so-called friend, or you simply let your dreams slip away through that third door. It's just easier right?

But is it really?

What would it be like to walk over to one of the other doors, turn the knob, and take a step inside?

Could some things be more difficult there? Possibly. It's also possible it would be temporarily harder, and then the most amazing things could happen. Or the most amazing things could happen right away. We just don't know unless we take a chance on choosing another door. The point is sometimes taking the risk to find out what is behind another option IS the best thing to do. When we process our feelings about what it is that doesn't feel right in our life, that's when we are able to see not only are there other choices available to us, but that's when we will find the courage to take steps for change.

We are in control of our own destiny. We just have to make the choice to create the outcome we desire.

KEY FOR CHANGE

Sit quietly with your eyes closed and begin to imagine a life that is what makes you happy in every category. What details are involved in this? Pay attention to any thoughts that come into your mind, you'll want to make a note of them in your journal. What does it feel like to imagine these wild and wonderful dreams? Describe the emotions. Let yourself feel them as if the things you envision are actually happening. Use these emotions in a short daily meditation where you see all the things you hope and dream of. Having a clear vision of what you want in addition to really experiencing the associated feelings will help you move toward the life you want. Believe deeply you are worthy of all the goodness you desire.

CHAPTER 13

BRAVERY OVER BUBBLE WRAP

*Too many of us are not living our dreams
because we are living our fears*

~ Les Brown, *Facebook, April 12, 2014*

Running is a big part of my life. I am an endurance runner, I enjoy the challenge of a marathon or an ultramarathon, especially on trails in the woods. Participating in this sport, of course, has some dangers associated with it. Things like wildlife encounters with rattlesnakes, copperheads, or bears, various stinging insects, and my most dreaded in the woods fear, ticks.

With the territory of this sport also comes possible injury. After a year where I experienced two significant physically damaging events, my friends began joking I should be wrapped in Bubble Wrap.

It's tempting to want to go through life living in metaphorical Bubble Wrap where we do what is comfortable and known, but the catch in that is we never move ourselves forward. We never grow, or really find out who we are and what we are meant to do. We might feel safe, but if we really evaluate where we are and ask ourselves some questions, it's likely we will see we are not truly comfortable with the results of staying rooted in one place.

I had a few people tell me they would be fearful of even going out again after having an injury like the one I sustained to my right hand which had me in a cast, then a surgery, followed by another cast, and then physical therapy and trying to regain the use of my hand. While I was afraid of being hurt again, my desire to experience the joy of doing what I love pushed me to go back out there and run again.

The idea of wrapping myself in Bubble Wrap to protect me from any hidden dangers, sounded appealing. In the end, it felt more appealing to me to leave the fear behind and go back out and experience my hobby fully again. At first, I didn't really leave the fear behind, I brought it along for the ride until I could gradually feel myself relaxing. For a while, I wore a brace on my hand, then when winter came and my gloves wouldn't fit over the brace, I started to tape both of my hands, thinking just in case I fell I would have a little support to provide protection.

It was like taking baby steps. I was telling myself "I'll do this one thing to make me feel safe," and then I could take another step a little further away from the safe point. Kind of like when you learn how to ride a bike and you start with training wheels and then you graduate to Mom or Dad holding the back of the bike. Eventually, they take their hand off the seat and just run close behind and before you know it, you are off on your own flying down the sidewalk in freedom.

In no time, riding that bike feels so second nature you are almost surprised you were ever afraid to begin with.

Fear is only a roadblock to happiness, so I choose a different perspective. This perspective says to me if I am fearful, I will live a small life, I will live like a tiny boat in a glass bottle. Restricted and compact. Think about that analogy... visualize a tiny sailboat inside a glass bottle sitting on a shelf. Now think about what happens to that bottle. Dust settles on the outside of it, and it never goes anywhere, it never sees anything new, never experiences anything. Now imagine a boat on the open water, it can go anywhere and can see limitless things.

If you're saying, "Well, the boat on the shelf is safe, it's not going to get hurt," I challenge you this, one day someone comes along and knocks it off the shelf, the glass breaks, and the boat falls to pieces. So, while it was living its "safe" life on the shelf, was it really any safer?

The George Addair quote "everything you've ever wanted is sitting on the other side of fear" is so very true. Do not be a tiny boat in a glass bottle staying stuck in your comfort zone. Instead, venture out into the growth zone and live in the open water, and experience all the beauty in life. Even if you have to wear your life vest for a while first.

We can get stuck in a loop of fear because when we have an experience and it doesn't go well, our brain tells us every time we try that thing, it's going to always happen that way. This is again why it's important when we have traumatic, difficult, or painful experiences in our lives, we must take the time to acknowledge and process our emotions.

While it might feel true things will always be the same, it isn't. However, our thoughts are powerful, and when we continue to tell ourselves that same story, the story does have a tendency to repeat itself. For example, saying "I'm bad at math" over and over begins a story that says you aren't capable of doing math, thus creating a block to learning it. I struggled with math all through school, but as an adult, I've found while it's definitely not my strongest skill, I am certainly capable of doing it. I had to start telling myself I could instead of continually telling the old story I was bad at it.

Have you ever noticed you might go down the same road every single day, but it can look different?

If you haven't noticed this, every day for a week take a short walk down the same road and pay attention to your surroundings. Even better, if you can do it at different times of the day, maybe even take a note of a few things, the colors you see and the way the light is, the people you might encounter, the temperature, the way the air feels, anything you might smell. Maybe even take pictures of the same things on different days. At the end of the week, compare and ask yourself was this ever the same road twice?

Experiences in life can be that way too. At the outset, they may be similar, but the details are different. We may have a friend, and one day they may turn on us, or we may have been in a relationship and found out they were an abuser, these things get stuck in our heads and begin to tell us every time we try that activity, or make a friend, or fall in love, the results will be the same. But that is not true. Oftentimes, and hopefully most of the time, we learn something from those experiences, and we will go into them with a new perspective. That new perspective is what will help us have a different experience.

If we tell ourselves over and over those experiences will be the same, our experience most likely will be the same. But if we tell ourself the story can change, it will. What we put out comes back to us. Focus your energy on what you DO want and not what you don't want.

If you want a different ending, you must put out a different energy.

I was talking to a woman one day who said, "I make myself small." The beautiful thing was, she recognized it, and she decided to do something about it. She wanted to take a trip, but all the people who were going to go with her backed out, so she decided she was going to just take her dog and go on her own.

Having a little adventure by yourself can be tremendously helpful for building self-confidence and showing yourself, you are capable of doing scary things. She stepped out of her comfort zone, left her fear behind, and went on the trip. She ended up having an amazing experience which helped her grow as a person.

Our imagination can create both limitations and wide-open possibilities, and the choice is ours. If we let our imagination settle on the good outcomes, we have a greater chance of having those. When we imagine negative outcomes, we often stop ourselves from pursuing something before we even get started. Perhaps if we let our mind be that of innocence and hope and not let our fears carry us away, we will have greater choices and experiences in our lives.

I'm not suggesting things that will put us in danger. I just mean it's helpful if we look at things for their possibilities rather than their limitations.

About twenty years ago, my then husband and I received a gift certificate to go up in an untethered hot air balloon. I wasn't really sure how I felt about doing this. I had some mix of excitement and terror about it, but somehow, I got in the basket, and I still remember so clearly how frightened I felt as the balloon took us higher and higher, and the people below us got smaller and smaller while we were floating away in a basket barely big enough to hold another couple and the pilot. As we floated upward, I could have taken that spark of fear and panicked, but instead, I leaned into the fear (figuratively and literally). As I began leaning out a bit to take pictures, I felt myself relax and begin to really enjoy the views and the experience. Sometimes this is what we need to do, we need to lean into the fear instead of pulling away and trying to put ourselves back into the glass bottle on the shelf.

When I first graduated from college and my new husband and I moved to the Washington, DC area, I didn't have a job yet, and I didn't know anyone. He had a job and was going into the city each day for work while I stayed at our apartment and applied for jobs. After a few weeks of this, I decided I was going to challenge my fear of living in a new place, and I went to the metro station by myself, headed into the city, and did a bunch of touristy things on my own. It was fun and empowering to realize I didn't actually need someone to "hold my hand" to go do things. I have tried to keep doing things that make me nervous, fearful, or anxious whenever possible, because what I have found is some of my greatest adventures have happened when I lean just a bit further into the fearful feeling.

Sometimes we have to speak to the fear. Literally ask the emotion of fear questions. You can do this, again, by accessing your subconscious mind, which, remember, is the keeper of your feelings; including fear. The next time you find yourself afraid, close your eyes and imagine you can talk to your fear. Ask it, "What do you need to tell me?" Then wait for a thought to arise. Maybe you are afraid of the outcome in a situation and how you would handle a significant change in your life. Maybe you are afraid of getting hurt physically or emotionally. Maybe it's a fear of abandonment or judgment. So, looking at the fears, it's not really the fear itself we need to confront, it's the reason behind it. For example, "What will happen if someone judges me for the choice I make?" Or "What will happen if I get lost driving across the country?"

What we really need to process is the possible outcomes. We need to look at what could happen and how we would handle it. If we let our imagination be in control, we will likely feel like something will be much worse than it actually is. When we can process the feelings surrounding the fear, we can approach things with a clear mind. Every time we do this, we are ensuring we don't create bars to a cage.

About fifteen years ago, my high school French class pen pal invited me to meet her in New York City. She and I had written letters to each other for years, sending cards and photos and gifts back-and-forth ever since tenth grade. I'm actually still in touch with her today at fifty years old, thanks to Facebook. Side note: even though I'm thankful to still be in touch, truth be told, I enjoyed writing those regular letters even more than just popping onto social media. There was something so exciting about receiving one of those old fashioned "air mail" envelopes! (That's not a story about fear though, just a happy memory, which also lives in my subconscious mind.)

She was going to visit her aunt in New York City, and said, "How about if you come and meet me?" To her it probably seemed simple, as I remember when she visited me when we were in high school, and she wanted to see inside a bar, and I told her we couldn't go in because we were underage. She looked at me, confused, and she simply turned around, opened the door, and walked in. I was so impressed with her boldness and lack of fear to do what "we shouldn't do," it left a lasting impression on me. Again, I'm not suggesting doing things that will put you in danger, just things you may have created false stories about what the outcome would be.

The idea of heading to New York City alone felt terrifying to me. It seemed a million miles away and busy and scary. In reality, it was about a four-hour drive but, indeed, was busy and scary! I had been there many times before, but never by myself. A ton of questions went through my mind. "How will I get there?" "What if I get lost?" "Won't this be uncomfortable?" "Should I really go do this?" At that time in my life, I struggled with anxiety, so this seemed extra challenging.

I certainly didn't want to drive there, but I really wanted to go despite being nervous about it. When I was about ten,

I remember my mom driving her sister, my two cousins, my grandmother, my brother, and I all to NYC to take my aunt to the airport. I had a strong memory of the traffic and how crazy it all seemed. I'd been there with others who had driven before, too, but it still felt daunting to me. I started thinking of other ways to get there, and I found out there was a shopping bus trip leaving from my town that day, and I could ride there, and instead of going shopping, go meet up with my friend. So, at about 4 a.m., I boarded a bus headed to the Big Apple on a big adventure.

It may seem like a small thing, but it scared me, and I did it anyway. It was so liberating, so exciting, and I was incredibly proud of myself for stepping out of my comfort zone.

Not only did I enjoy a fun trip to New York City, catching up with my old friend, but it also opened new and exciting doors for me. This one small action showed me I did not have to do things the way I always had done before. I'm now completely comfortable flying across the country myself, getting Uber rides or renting cars, and exploring new things on my own, though I'd still probably not want to drive to New York City!

Sometimes, we need to surrender.

Have you ever tried to put an unwilling dog into a bathtub for a bath? If you have, you surely understand what I'm saying when I say resistance makes things so much harder. That little dog could make itself seem thirty pounds heavier by resisting putting its paws in the water. We do this to ourselves as well, the more we resist change or letting go of control, the harder things are. If we allow ourselves to flow with life, everything happens with ease. When we can step into a place of surrender knowing the universe has our best interest at heart, things will always work out exactly how they are meant to. Does that mean you will like the results every time? No, of course not, but what it means is you will learn what you're meant to learn and will be where you are meant to be.

On a recent trail run, I was thinking about how I'm so much better at the climbs than the downhills. There's something about the downhill that scares me. Maybe it's the lack of control and having to just let go. Even though I feel I've been working on this for a very long time, there are still moments where just letting go and letting things be seems so much harder than working and working at what you want. The irony is the surrender in the downhill gets you to the finish line faster. When we stop trying to control or resist the changes in life, we actually stop suffering, we trust the process of moving forward, and things change.

When we begin to accept we cannot control the outcome of every situation, it makes life easier by allowing us to relax and observe what's happening knowing we can bring our knowledge and effort to a situation. But most often, there are other people involved, and we can't always control what they bring—or don't bring. My friend Cynthia has a saying I love, she says "My ingredients, not the outcome."

If you think about baking a cake, we mix up the required ingredients, and put them into a pan, then place the pan in the oven where the heat and time will do their job. When we open the oven, we might see a perfectly baked cake, or one that didn't rise quite right. There are always variables to this equation. I've baked before only to find out my baking powder was expired, or the oven wasn't set right, or I didn't hear the timer go off, and what I had hoped to see upon opening the oven door was not what was there. I brought my ingredients, but I couldn't completely control the outcome. Sometimes, we get perfect results and that feels great. Other times, the results are less than optimal, and we learn something. Either way, it's a win and likely exactly what we needed in the end.

We often say we want something, but our actions may contradict that. We hold ourselves back with the fear of the unknown. We cannot be fully present in a room if we always have one foot back on the other side of the threshold. We need to look at what it is that is stopping us from confidently stepping with our whole selves and our whole hearts into a place we desire to be.

I think surrender is a big part of making positive change. In childbirth, there comes a point where the pain is no longer able to stop what your body will naturally do. The stage of transition is the most painful part of giving birth. It's when everything intensifies. The contractions are harder and longer, there is very little relief between them. The only option is to surrender to the process. To move through it, and eventually, to make the final effort to push your baby out. And then, just like that, the reward is there. What a beautiful metaphor for healing this is. We have to really put ourselves into the most painful part of an experience in order to release ourselves from whatever is holding us back. The joy and relief then bring us freedom.

My youngest son Nick hiked the Camino de Santiago

in Spain this past summer. It's a 500-mile trek from Saint-Jean-Pied-de-Porte at the base of the Pyrenees in France to Santiago de Compostela in Spain. When he shared he wanted to embark on this journey, I, of course, wanted to learn all I could about it, so I would know what he was going to experience. I watched videos, read books, and began following Facebook pages for Pilgrims, which is what one who does this walk is called. On those Facebook pages, there are lots of posts about what to bring with you, how much your pack should weigh, what was useful, and what was not. I paid extra attention to those posts, so I could be involved and help my son figure out what he would want to pack. Reading a thread one day, someone said they ended up mailing home five extra pounds of things they decided they didn't need once they started. People asked, "What did you send home?" They replied with various items like an additional change of clothes, a metal coffee cup, too many medical supplies, etc. They followed up by commenting "As they say, don't carry your fears." How profound is that? How much extra "stuff" do we carry through life that is based in fear?

KEY FOR CHANGE

So, how do we do it? How do we lean into fear and indeed gently put it down and see what opportunity lies on the other side of that heavy obstacle?

To begin with, it's always helpful to ask yourself just what it is you are afraid of in the first place. Is it getting lost? Is it failing? Is it being rejected? Try writing down the answers to those questions.

If the fear is of failing, ask yourself next what would be a failure in this situation? When we confront our fears, it's like taking them out of a dark box and bringing them out into the light where we can turn them around and see them from all sides. Things are much less frightening when we really examine and understand just what it is that is holding us back. When we see what good can come from trying or doing something that makes us feel afraid, everything seems possible.

CHAPTER 14

Say Woah to Woe is Me

*Your transformation will begin the moment you
stop waiting for someone else to rescue you.*

~ John Mark Green, *Facebook, January 25, 2024*

Have you ever felt like everyone was out to get you and nothing ever went right for you? Did you think you didn't have any control over improving your situation? Were you ignoring any advice or help that was offered? Keep these questions in mind as you read this chapter.

There are many stages, steps, and layers to healing, and one of them for some people is realizing we are not a victim, but rather a resilient thriver in our story. How that story plays out is all up to us. What we put out is what comes back to us. When we live in a negative place in our mind, negativity will continue to find us. We cannot expect to have a positive life if all we focus on is what is going wrong.

It is easy to fall into the "victimhood" trap especially if we've had a lot of traumas in our lives. I hesitate to even use the word "victim" to describe this mindset because of this, but with awareness, we can step out of it. It all begins with processing our emotions, as has been the theme throughout this book. When we have fully felt and experienced our feelings, we aren't left with this misguided idea the world is conspiring against us. Yes, bad things may have happened in our lives, but they don't have to define us. We will take our control back, and we will instead embrace the growth and blessings our challenges bring us.

Earlier, I discussed positivity and why before we can be positive, we must look into and process through our negative emotions. I mentioned those people who are always on social media posting about their woes and all of the bad things that happen to them. They are likely stuck in the aftermath of their past traumas. Talking about bad things that happen to them becomes commonplace for them. It's almost as if they get some sort of satisfaction from constantly sharing everything that is wrong in their life, and in a strange way, they actually might be. It's unlikely that this is intentional on their part, but rather the result of unprocessed negative emotions.

In some instances, we are receiving some kind of secondary gain from doing so. A secondary gain is any advantage we obtain from holding onto a negative behavior or situation. We might get a lot of attention from always having a problem. This can confuse us and make it seem as though it's a good thing to always have something bad happening to us. We may enjoy the comfort or recognition we get from having a need for help or for having yet another bad thing plaguing us. It can become addictive, though most often, we are not aware we are receiving a gain and are truly in distress, but subconsciously, we may be almost creating these negative experiences just so we have something to talk about or get sympathy for.

If you find yourself in a cycle of "woe is me," ask yourself "Is there some positive thing I get from always having something going wrong in my life?" If we can identify we are doing this, it makes it easier to break the cycle. Once we realize there is actually way more good to be had from focusing on the positives, we can begin to step away from victimhood. This doesn't mean you haven't had difficult things happen, which are all valid and deserve to be addressed and processed, it just means that you are now willing to integrate what you've learned from those experiences and allow yourself to begin feeling better. Take a moment and repeat these words: "I am allowed to feel better." Take a deep breath, exhale, and say the words a second time. "I am allowed to feel better."

Some signs of a victim mentality are:

- Always focusing on negative things that happen
- Repeating negative stories over and over
- Believing everything is hard in your life
- Blaming others for what is wrong in your life
- Always finding a reason why solutions to your problems won't work
- Believing you will never get ahead
- Having a glass half empty attitude
- Being judgmental
- Lacking empathy for others
- Thinking everyone else has it easier than you

These are just some thoughts and attitudes expressed by those living in a victim mode. If you recognize any of these statements or beliefs being repeated by you, don't worry, you can change that. It will be necessary to look inward, to ask yourself why you are feeling this way. **There are reasons you feel this way.** What have you experienced that created these thought patterns for you? It is possible to change, but requires courage to move into action to take control back.

Those people always posting the negative things on social media or constantly having a list of what is wrong in their life might get a lot of attention from this for a while, which creates the secondary gain. In time, they get fewer and fewer people to comment or to like their posts, and then that also becomes a part of the negative story—compounding what they've already been telling themselves.

Their thoughts may go to things like "Look no one even cares enough to comment." Maybe you've also seen as time after time people offer help and guidance to the person, but they never follow through with any of it, always having some reason why they can't and instead choose to stay in that negative space. It's like the meme with a man on a roof as flood water is rising, and he cries out to God, "Help me please!" God sends a fisherman in a boat, and the man on the roof declines the rescue saying he is waiting for God to come and then asks God again for help. Soon a helicopter appears, and the man also turns down that ride. Finally, the man cries "God, why didn't you help me?" And God says, "I sent a boat and a helicopter!" Sometimes we just can't let ourselves see the opportunity in front of us because we have a cloud of negative feelings blocking the way.

I said this earlier, but it bears repeating, the subconscious mind loves what it's used to and what it knows, even when it's bad for us. In essence, it would rather subject itself to the same pain day after day rather than have a different and unknown experience. The subconscious will work hard to keep us in the same old place because it knows and understands that place.

Awareness is the first step to transformation. We cannot change something if we don't know we are doing it. So often, we are fully engrossed in the narrative we have created for ourselves that we have blinders on. We don't even realize we are telling a story that isn't true, because the old familiar feeling we had is there with us, so it feels normal and comfortable. Introspection is a powerful tool to begin to make changes. We really need to spend time in our own minds and with our own hearts asking what is true and what is a story we have created to fit the old feelings.

When we are in a victim mindset, we are in essence giving away our power. We are giving it away to the emotions of past negative events, that are keeping us locked in a cage of anger, blame, and resentment.

KEY FOR CHANGE

How to shift from a victim mindset:

Ask yourself some questions and be as honest as possible.

- Do I look at the negative side of everything?
- Am I always believing my life is hard and I can't get ahead?

- Do I shut down any suggestions for ways to make my situation better?

- If you answered yes to any of these, consider the following:

  1. Process negative emotions from past events. Your feelings are valid, things have happened in your life to create them, however, they do not have to cage or control you.

  2. Take responsibility for your actions and your life. This doesn't mean excusing ways people hurt you. It means accepting you ultimately have control of your life because you can create boundaries, and yes, offer forgiveness, to yourself and others.

  3. Look for the good in situations and begin to train your brain to make that your first thought rather than focusing on the bad.

Flip the Script

We all have a story we tell ourselves about who we are and what our life is like. The really amazing thing is we have the power to choose what that story is. We can choose a story of victimhood, scarcity, pain, and sadness, or we can choose a story of confidence, peace, abundance, and joy. You can start right now with the exact story you have lived your whole life and decide to make a change. Just because you may have had bad things happen in your life—and let's face it, who hasn't?—doesn't mean you can't have a beautiful story for your present, and your future.

We have the ability to talk ourselves into or out of anything. In fact, I was struggling with writing this book and suddenly realized I was telling myself I was struggling, and so it felt harder and harder where only days before I was literally dreaming the words to write, and it all came pouring out of me. What had happened to make that change so drastically for me? When I hit a small patch of difficult writing, I started running a loop in my mind that said, "This is hard" and "Nothing is coming to me." The more I played this loop, the more real it became. I started doubting I could even finish the book, even though I was about halfway through writing it at that point. I was telling myself there was nothing left for me to say, even though deep down, I knew this to be false. As I opened the page in my book I had previously set up called "change the story you tell yourself," it hit me I was telling myself a story that wasn't true, or that didn't have to be true. It didn't have to be hard to get the book finished, I merely had to change my narrative. Not the narrative of the book, but the narrative in my mind.

Whatever we set in our minds tends to become true for us. Don't believe me? Test it out. If you've ever told yourself you couldn't do something, did that become true? Conversely, try telling yourself you CAN do something. Even go a step farther and start feeling like you've already done it, and soon enough, you will have completed that very thing. Dr. Joe Dispenza, author of *Break the Habit of Being Yourself* and *Becoming Supernatural* among others is a well-known teacher of quantum healing and using meditation to create anything you want in life. He is an incredible example of the power of telling the story you want to be yours and finding yourself with those very results. He himself proved it to be true after being hit by a car while riding his bike in a triathlon and broke six vertebrae. Doctors wanted him to have risky surgery that could have left him handicapped. Instead, Joe decided in the time he was lying flat for months to use the power of his mind to heal his body. He visualized himself healed and back to normal. He went a step further and created the emotions as if it were already true. He began living in that space in his mind, with his emotions already on the result he wanted, believing it had already happened. Just nine weeks later, he was healed and back to training three weeks after that. The mind has incredible power to create our reality.

Another example to consider. How often do you say the phrase "I don't have time" or "I would do that, but I'm too busy"? The more you say it, the more it becomes true. Whatever we tell ourselves over and over, we begin to believe. The more we believe it, the more it continues. As with any mindset change, again, the first step is awareness. We cannot change anything if we are not aware we are doing something. Notice when you are saying you don't have time and also begin to notice when you are spending time doing things that do not line up with your desires and goals. You are creating that reality by allowing yourself to be distracted and pulled away from your goals by putting your focus in the wrong place. It might be time to ask yourself some questions to see if the goal really is important to you or if you are sabotaging yourself. For example, if you feel you don't have time to reach a goal, ask yourself is this true? What is the real reason I feel I don't have time? It could be the goal is really not important to you after all, or you are pursuing it for the wrong reasons. It could be fear, or something else altogether, but first you must be aware of the story, then you must begin to consider and process your feelings so that you can write a new story that is the truth for you.

KEY FOR CHANGE

Change the story

Think about a story you tell yourself about your life, and really get honest with yourself about the reasons why you tell this story.

As always it helps to write these reasons down. Reading them will help you connect to the feelings behind them.

If the story is the absolute truth and you don't believe you can change it, decide if you are accepting this story or if you want to choose a new story. The power to change anything is within us. Start with awareness of the story, then begin looking inward at how you feel about it. Your new, better story is as close as that.

CHAPTER 15

PERFECT SCHMERFECT

At its root, perfectionism isn't really about
a deep love of being meticulous. It's about fear.
Fear of making a mistake. Fear of disappointing
others. Fear of failure. Fear of success.

~Michael Law, *Facebook, March 25, 2021*

The board game Perfection came out the year I was born (1973 in case you are a trivia buff). I think this is apropos considering I've struggled with perfectionism throughout my life. This game was nothing but an anxiety creator, also appropriate to its name, and what perfectionism does. In the game, you push down an ejector plate, set a timer, and must fit assorted shapes into their assigned places as quickly as possible. If you didn't beat the timer, thereby being perfect, the whole thing exploded, and all the work you did was for nothing. I remember anxiously trying to hurry though the game and feeling so disappointed when I didn't get it right.

Kinda like what trying to attain perfection in life feels like, isn't it? Anxiety and disappointment. Yuck.

We develop perfectionistic tendencies because we have things happen that create a story within us that says we must be this way or else there will be consequences that are not desirable. We begin to believe this is the truth, and we will continue in patterns that perpetuate the desire for perfection as a coping mechanism.

Imagine a little girl, I'll call her Anna, hearing her parents arguing. She may not understand what they are fighting about, but she will hear the angry tones and feel the energy of their emotions. She may be hiding in her room as this goes on, and suddenly, she hears her name in this disagreement. She may take that little bit of information; the angry voices, her name being included in the outburst. She may then begin to feel like she has to be very, very good so that her parents don't argue again. She may take that little seed and let it grow with every time she worries about behaving enough or being good enough. After all, she doesn't want her parents to be angry or argue or get divorced. That feeling she has might begin to expand in other areas of her life. She might begin to think she has to be perfect so that things stay calm and happy in her home. This may become a very stressful way of existing for her. Her desire to be perfect is driven out of fear. She doesn't want anyone mad or disappointed in her. And so, perfectionism is born for her.

Now imagine, years later the little girl as an adult is struggling with this need to be so perfect she is stressed, anxious, and just plain tired from trying so hard to measure up to a standard no one actually set for her. A standard that in her subconscious mind was built from a tiny piece of information and from not having the tools at her young age to really work through her feelings in the moment.

What if she were able to go back in time to begin to find where this idea came from? What if in her search, she was led to that time she overheard the argument? What if now with her adult mind, she was able to understand what was going on at the time she heard her parents angry voices say her name? In this example, she remembers the details and is able to see her parents were arguing about money. That her dad was angry because her mom was shopping and over-drew their bank account. He was upset. Her mom was angry with her dad because he was supposed to transfer money to that account so that her mom could take the little girl school clothes shopping. Her dad asked her mom, "What did you buy?" and her mom said, "I bought shoes for Anna."

How might that information have made a change in Anna's life? She might suddenly see it wasn't about her at all. No one was mad at her, no one expected perfection from her. She just didn't understand and used being perfect as a way to cope with the stress she felt in that moment, and that was likely compounded over time in many other circumstances. That first event was just the seed that grew into a way of doing things that wasn't healthy or helpful to her. It was the initial sensitizing event, which was likely followed by other situations over time.

Have you ever been on a job interview, and they ask you the dreaded question, what is your greatest strength AND your greatest weakness? I remember once responding with the word "perfectionism" to both questions. I feel like this is a cliché answer, but at the time, fresh out of college with no real experience, I didn't know what else to say. It was true, perfectionism in many ways felt like a blessing and a curse. While trying to do things perfectly can end up making some great successes, the emotional cost of it can be quite intense if you are unable to appreciate your effort regardless of the results.

I believe in doing one's best in all things, however, the healthy way to do this is to understand that one's best can change day to day, or even from one hour to the next. If you've literally given all you have to give to a project on a particular day, but it happens to be less than it was the day before, have you not given your best? Of course, you have. It may be on that day, you were having a migraine, or you had not gotten much sleep, or you were worried about a sick parent or child. The point is if you have done what you can do in a day, it is your best. The next day might produce greater results, and that means you gave your best that day too.

Unfortunately, though, we spend a lot of time striving for something we already have in the hopes of feeling loved and accepted. We look outside ourselves to feel complete, and the problem with that is nothing outside ourselves can ever do that.

When I go for a run, I try to make my runs in particular distances. For example, 3.1, 5, 6.2, 10, 13.1 miles, etc., which are either regular race distances or nice rounded numbers. It's a habit I have, and that many runners I know have. Something about the solid distance is really satisfying. One day, I was thinking about this kind of "obsession" with rounding the numbers as I was trying to figure out how to make it exactly 5. I started thinking about what would happen if I stopped doing that and let the runs end where they would, a little bit more than the distance a little bit less than the distance. What would happen at the end of the year, would my mileage end up being the same because I didn't try so hard to make it all perfect? Probably.

One day, a friend saw my run was an odd distance, and she texted me she thought it was really badass I didn't make it so perfect. I got to thinking about that and what that meant. When you are a perfectionist, breaking away from the nice orderly numbers is so much harder, but being a badass seems so much more appealing than having to have everything so ridiculously perfect. How freeing that can be!

What about in the rest of life, if we just stop trying to make everything so neat and tidy and just let things be, would the results be better? I don't mean stop doing the things you need to take care of your family, your home, your job, or whatever else you might find yourself obsessing over. What I mean is what if you stopped focusing on making sure everything was just so, especially if it is being done at a sacrifice to your well-being. Could you clean your house a little each day rather than trying to accomplish it all in one day? Could you make healthy meals quickly that don't have to be new and exciting every week, but as long as they are giving your family and your body what is needed, would that be ok? My mom always said, "It doesn't have to be hard to be good"—this has stuck with me when I'm trying to come up with something new to cook or when completing a project. I ask myself if I'm making it harder than it needs to be, the answer is often yes. We don't have to be a gourmet cook, keep our house meticulous all the time, or constantly try to make everyone happy by over delivering in all situations. We can just do our best that day, that hour, that moment, and know we are and always have been good enough.

As with all of the mindset changes I'm suggesting, we must first look at, analyze, and process our feelings if we want to be truly free. One of the best ways to impact the need to be perfect is to believe in your heart you are good enough exactly as you are. A self-worth and self-care practice will help greatly. So many of our issues in life go back to needing to believe in ourself and our worth.

It's certainly ok to have preferences in how we do things, and to want things to be done correctly and well. The problem really arises when the need for perfectionism harms you in some way. Whether it keeps you stuck because you are fearful of not completing something well, or if it drains your energy because you are constantly re-doing things, or if it has you living in fear of the "what ifs" of something not going "perfectly."

Can you indulge me with bearing with one more running reference. (Ok, in this chapter if I'm being honest with you, I can't promise the subject won't come up again within these pages!)

Apply these anecdotes to whatever it is you find yourself trying to get "perfect" with. I'm using running, because it's definitely an area I have struggled with a desire for perfection, it's been a place I've looked for validation to feel that "good enough" feeling we all desire. It's taught me many lessons in my life, and the next story illustrates how it let me push the boundary of what I thought I was comfortable with and loosened my grip on perfect just a little more.

I cover a lot of miles each year. Some years are more than others depending on races I sign up for and the occasional injury. A few years ago, I was noticing running friends posting their mileages for the year, and I wondered where mine was. Though I had not ever made a conscious effort to track them, I was curious and checked the app connected to my fitness watch to see where I was. I was surprised to see with two weeks left in the year, I had run 1333.97 miles.

When I saw that, my first thought was not "Wow, I ran over 1000 miles."

My first thought was look how close I was to 1500!

Ugh. Why? Why is the first thought always to look at what we haven't done rather than to applaud what we have done?

I tried for the next two weeks to get as many miles as I could within reason and consideration of the fact December is always a busy month, and I also didn't want to risk getting hurt. I just wanted to see where I'd end up. As it got closer to the last day of the year, I kept checking in on my number. On New Year's Eve, I decided to do something fun because I was still going to be short of a 1500-mile end number. I finished my run at 1399.9. That felt really good. I just let it be at that point, and it was liberating. It was time to look at what I HAD done and not what I had failed to do.

About a dozen years ago, I had a show of my jewelry and photographs at a local art gallery. I had taken twenty photographs and designed a piece of jewelry inspired by each photo for each one. I wrote a little description of every photo and jewelry piece to illustrate the place of inspiration in each. One was a photograph entitled *Alive*. The image was of a fountain in Siena, Italy. It had very detailed sculptures of people sitting around the fountain with blue-green water below. There were pigeons perched on the sculptures, and in the photograph I took, one pigeon had just taken flight, wings spread, lifting away from the marble. I thought it was interesting how the bird in flight created a juxtaposition against the inanimate sculptures that upon a second look appear to be crying as the marble was stained in what looked like tears rolling down their faces. Then the bird, full of life, wings spread taking off into the sky.

The title *Alive* felt so appropriate as the bird was taking its freedom and soaring. The jewelry piece that went with this was of a bird flying out of the bars of a cage. I called this piece, not ironically, *Free from the Cage*. The bird was breaking out of his cage to live his life. As I saw the stone people in the photograph unable to do. Of course, I know this is a sculpture, but I like to see the metaphors in things as you have surely learned about me as you have been reading this book. It helps me have a clearer perspective. The bird was taking flight as any oppressed person may want to do but might feel frozen or stuck and, therefore, unable to do. Essentially living in a cage of their own creation. It was intended as a joyful piece. My desire was to have the wearer feel like they could break the bars of their cage and truly fly too. While working on this book, one day, I saw very clearly that piece of jewelry in my mind, and knew that was the title of the book. The bars of the cage were created by negative emotions, and in order to be free, we need to feel those feelings, so the door can open and we can fly.

We can be free from perfectionism by looking at why we feel the need to be this way. We can examine our fear of failure, of letting others down, of not being good enough, and instead, realize each and every day doing our best is what we should strive for, not an unrealistic and unattainable standard that only cages us in.

KEY FOR CHANGE

It's important to ask yourself the real reason you feel the need to be perfect and work through any associated feelings.

Here are some other things you can do to begin to shift your mindset from perfection to progress and simply doing your best in the moment you are currently in.

- Set attainable and realistic goals for where you are in your life at this time.

- If you find yourself trying to go back to something you already deemed complete, stop, take a deep breath, and say, *"It's already done and it's done well."* Resist the urge to redo or overdo something. Praise yourself when you do.

- It might help to give yourself time limits for tasks you tend to stress over. It will help you not only be more efficient, but also give you a defined stopping point which in time will assist you in making sure your expectations are realistic.

- Letting perfectionism go challenge: Find an area you tend to over deliver on. For example, if you have been asked to bake something for your child's school bake sale, and normally you would bake and individually package cookies and tie beautiful ribbons with tags on each and place in a hand-woven basket, try just baking the cookies (or even buying some from the store if you want to get really crazy!) and then drop them off in Ziploc bags.

- Practice completing a task in a way that says, "I met the requirements and even did a very nice job," but don't miss out on sleep hand lettering cards if you could easily print something out.

Try it, see how free you feel and notice nothing bad happened when you did things a little differently. You'll be amazed at how free you feel!

CHAPTER 16

HOW DID THAT GET IN THERE?

If you accept a limiting belief,
then it will become a truth for you

~Louise Hay, *Modern-Day Miracles*

A limiting belief is a thought or opinion of ourself that restricts us in some way. These beliefs will hold us back from achieving goals, growing, trying new things, or embracing new opportunities. Limiting beliefs are often formed in childhood, usually from birth to about age seven. These ideas are formed in our subconscious mind about who we are and what we believe. The influences come from our authority figures, such as our parents, grandparents, older siblings, teachers, clergy members, etc. We take in what is going on around us and begin to see a picture of ourselves. However, this picture may not be accurate, especially if some of the people we are looking up to are wounded and lost themselves. We may then be repeating patterns we see them repeating, in essence, following an outdated map and wondering why we are not getting to our desired destination.

As children, we are watching, we are listening, and we are taking in what we believe to be true based on what we observe and what we experience. The problem is our minds are not fully developed at that time and cannot completely understand some concepts or situations. Then conclusions are drawn from various events, and those conclusions create beliefs which become engrained in us even if they are not true.

We may be carrying around beliefs because of something we heard and misinterpreted as a child, or something we observed an authority figure doing and took it on as our own truth even if it feels wrong to us. Likewise, someone may have said something to us in anger such as "You are bad!" Or "You'll never amount to anything!" which may then have us believing those negative ideas and therefore create limiting beliefs within our mind.

Here are some examples of limiting belief statements we may find ourselves using:

- "I am not worthy of being loved."
- "Bad things always happen to me."
- "I am not smart/pretty/talented enough."
- "People won't like the real me."
- "I don't have enough time/experience/resources to pursue my passion."
- "I should avoid failure at all costs."
- "I can't catch a break."
- "People will always hurt me."
- "I don't know what I want."

- "I don't like my body."
- "I'll never measure up."
- "Life is hard, that's just how it is."
- "There's too much competition."
- "I have no choice."
- "I better not express my feelings if I want to be loved and accepted."
- "I just have bad luck."
- "Getting my hopes up always leads to disappointment."
- "I can't trust myself."
- "I'll never be successful."
- "I'm afraid of trying and failing."

Limiting beliefs can also be created after childhood when we are presented with a situation that causes us pain. Our subconscious mind will analyze the event, draw conclusions about it, and come up with a way to protect itself so that this pain is not felt again. We can become quite paralyzed by this. Our limiting beliefs can become controlling and might keep us from seeing opportunities or prevent us from even trying at all.

When I was in college, I had a car accident. My stepsister was graduating from high school that day in New Jersey, and I was attending school at Penn State. At that time, I was working in the campus bakery in the early hours of the day before going to classes. I planned to work my shift and then drive home and be able to ride with my mom and stepdad to New Jersey. I was heading toward the bakery at five a.m. and realized I was going to need gas for the trip later, so I decided to go to the gas station first. I went to pull out from a flashing red light, and I didn't see a truck coming quite fast up the road because some bushes obstructed my view. Before I knew what happened, our cars collided, and I watched him go out of control up the road about fifty yards. It was the strangest feeling, like everything was moving in slow motion. My body started shaking, and I could feel a rush of energy in my system. I had never experienced a car accident before, and it was so surreal.

I got out of my vehicle and ran down the road to check on the other driver, who was a man in his late sixties. I kept asking if he was ok, but all he did was yell at me, and tell me how stupid I was. His anger in the moment compounded my fear from the accident. He never did ask how I was, nor did he speak to me again once the police arrived. Both of our cars were totaled.

After that, I went from being very comfortable behind the wheel to being afraid to drive anywhere. I had anxiety about driving, and when a year later I got married and moved to the Washington, DC area, I became totally dependent on either public transportation or my husband to drive me places. I had never driven in a busy area like Northern VA where we lived or DC where we worked, and after my experience with the accident, I became paralyzed even thinking about getting in the driver's seat. I watched myself lose my independence and feel fearful about something I had always been comfortable with. When I was a teenager, I didn't think anything of driving a few towns away to do things with friends. Even though

I was new to driving, I didn't have a negative experience to cloud my view of driving. I'd never been a passenger in an accident, so it never even occurred to me it could happen. Until it did. Then everything changed. The more my fear grew, the more my limiting belief driving is dangerous was cemented in my subconscious mind. After a while, that belief was not only controlling me, but it allowed others to control me too. I was at everyone's mercy to get where I wanted to go, and aside from close to home grocery trips and things like that, I didn't ever want to drive. I eventually had to challenge that belief and get behind the wheel again. My husband and I were working in the same government building, and we commuted together for many years. So for a long time I didn't even need to think about driving. Then he changed jobs. I had to get comfortable with it again, and this time it was on the DC Beltway which in and of itself can be very scary! With four fast moving lanes in each direction, it was intimidating to say the least.

I decided in order to regain my freedom, I needed to face this story I was telling myself that was holding me back. I challenged my belief by remembering I had driven quite comfortably in the past, so why couldn't I do it again? I began to consider my options. If I didn't start driving myself, my world was about to get much smaller. I didn't like that idea, knowing it had already been impacted by my dependence on others to go places. I made myself face my uncomfortableness and get back behind the wheel, and I created a new belief. I told myself yes, accidents can happen, but they won't happen all the time, and it is safe to drive. Just like that, by asking myself some questions about what my fear was and then considering new possibilities and finally by testing them, I opened a cage I had created for myself with my limiting belief. Freedom feels good! Your imagination can create both limitations and wide-open possibilities. The choice is yours.

There was a time where I ran 5k races often and was somewhat competitive within the local field. One day I was running this 5K and was pushing pretty hard. Somewhere in the second mile, out of my peripheral I saw a woman approaching. She pushed ahead of me and passed me. I increased my pace, and then I passed her, and once again she moved ahead of me. This went on for about a mile. After a while, I felt like there was no way I could possibly get ahead of her and stay there. I told myself "What did it matter anyway, I'm tired, and I just can't do it." I stopped believing I could maintain my place.

Eventually, I turned and looked at her as she edged toward me, and I said, "You got me." I let her go ahead, and I felt everything inside me give up. She crossed the finish line. I crossed not too far behind her, and as I did, the woman taking our bib numbers looked at me and said, "Congratulations, you are the second female!" I looked at her with shock and said, (in between panting breaths), "The second female overall?" And she said, "Yes, you are the second female overall." I was so upset with myself in that moment, if only I had continued to try, I may have been first. If I had continued to try, and she still beat me, at least I would've known I had given it my all. In the end, I let fear and a false belief I couldn't possibly do well enough to finish ahead of this person defeat me. I don't know if I could've beaten her or not, but giving up like I did, assured I wouldn't. I had never come that close to being the first female finisher. When the race was over, I realized it wasn't I couldn't get ahead of her, I just stopped believing it was possible. I sabotaged my own success with a false belief I wasn't good enough.

My limiting belief I was out of energy and had nothing left to give stopped my success. Looking back at that event now, I wish I had just tried to push a little bit more, just to see what I was in fact capable of.

Somewhere in my mind, I told myself a story that said I couldn't do it. I wonder what would have happened if I had instead told myself "I could possibly win this race if I pushed just a little more."

I am not saying you should push yourself to exhaustion in life, or do something that could harm you, but I remember that day, and I remember I simply stopped trying. I let negative self-talk come in and tell me I couldn't do it. We can have limiting beliefs in many different areas of our lives, and those beliefs will be roadblocks to our success if we let them persist. You can start changing them today and work toward freedom to have, do, and be whatever you most desire.

KEY FOR CHANGE

Identify your limiting beliefs

Look at an area of your life and determine what you say to yourself about it. Is there a story you are telling yourself that is limiting your ability to achieve a dream you have?

For example, if you didn't get a promotion you really wanted, maybe you explain it away with something like:

"It would have been a lot more work and not much more money, I'm glad it didn't work out." Saying something like this just gives you permission or justification to stay stuck in your limiting belief.

EXERCISE: Can you name a limiting belief you may have? Write it down. Identifying it is the first step. You may have several. Making a list so you can see where you might be sabotaging your success or happiness will help you push toward creating beliefs that better support your goals and dreams.

Lose the Coat

So, how do we change these limiting beliefs?

If a limiting belief is a way of thinking that has our goal conflicting with our underlying belief in some way, then we must look at both the goal and the feelings behind the belief.

Imagine you have been walking around wearing a very heavy woolen or fur coat, and it's hot out. It's very hot. Yet you are still wearing this coat you don't need, but instead of taking it off, you snuggle into it because it's what you've always worn. You might feel oppressed by the weight of it, yet still feel hesitant to take it off because it's what you've always known.

Your discomfort may not even consciously register with you because you've become so used to it. But imagine now that suddenly you became aware of how warm it is in that coat and maybe you slip one arm out of the sleeve, and you feel how much cooler it is, but you feel afraid to let go of the coat. Now if you tested it even further and pull the other arm out, then imagine your surprise and elation to realize you can be comfortable even leaving something very familiar behind. This is what it is like to change a limiting belief. We suddenly have a new perspective, a new experience, indeed a new belief.

When we examine what we feel about a belief that is holding us back and determine if that feeling is based in truth or if it's just a story we've been telling and retelling, many new doors open for us.

When I was in middle school, we were allowed to start playing a musical instrument and receive music lessons at school. I was two years younger than my brother who had started playing trumpet when he was old enough but had recently quit his lessons, though he later went back to it and became an incredibly talented musician and learned several instruments as well as being an awesome vocalist. So, when the time to choose instruments came, my mom suggested I play trumpet because we already had one. I was typically an agreeable child, so I said I'd give it a try. I probably would have preferred saxophone or something else, but I was just happy to play something. I went to my lessons dutifully and practiced at home daily. I tried very hard to learn this instrument, but something wasn't clicking for me. The band instructor was a gruff man. I don't think I ever saw him smile. He seemed exceedingly unhappy, and every time I walked into his classroom, I felt a bit paralyzed with fear of him. The atmosphere made me so uncomfortable it was hard to focus. Luckily, I took lessons with two other kids, so it wasn't just me in there, but I was by far the least talented. One day, I guess the teacher had had enough of trying to deal with my poor musical ability, and he lost it and started yelling at me. He said, "You obviously don't practice!" To which I said with a quivering lip "But I do!" He was unmoved and then shouted, "You don't want to be here, you should just get out!" Fighting back tears, I stood and walked to where my trumpet case sat, knelt down and dissembled my instrument, placed it in its case, closed it, and without saying a word, turned and walked out the door. I never went back.

That experience created a limiting belief that was quite powerful for me. I believed from that moment on I was musically stupid, I couldn't possibly learn to play music. Even practicing was not worth doing because I still wouldn't be able to learn. The problem was I desperately wanted to learn! In high school, I asked my mom if I could try piano lessons. I also tried playing the marimba. It was a real struggle for me. I just couldn't seem to "get it." My brain had truly shut down to the idea. Into adulthood I always regretted not learning, and so often would tell people who asked if I played an instrument that "My brother got all the musical talent in our family." When my sons took music lessons, I loved watching them practice and hearing them play the saxophone, French horn, and bass, but was still feeling sad I never learned. I told myself I was musically inept, even though a piece of me longed to try again.

Fast forward a few decades and I became friends with Jack and Tammy, a couple who led drum circles with djembe drums. Djembe drums are wooden drums shaped kind of like a goblet and have animal skin pulled over the top and are fastened with rope. Drum circles are group gatherings organized to create a feeling of community and connection while relieving anxiety and stress through the release of endorphins in the brain. The drums are played with bare hands and the name djembe comes from the saying "Anke djé, anke bé" which translates to "everyone gather together in peace." Even the name sounded mystical and possible to me. When I attended one of their events, I was hooked. I didn't have to read music, just feel it. I remember one evening when they came to our house after a drum circle and my husband Mark and I and the two of them got our drums out. We were all just playing rhythms and letting things flow, and then one of them said we should try something more complex. I felt myself tighten up. It was one thing to just play what I felt but another to now fit in a particular rhythm in a small group when if I messed up, everyone would know it was me. Tears started welling up. I suddenly remembered being in that music room in middle school. I shared the story and said how much I always wanted to be a "musical" person. They were encouraging, and even though I was awkward with finding the flow, they were patient. We had a fun evening, and I began to realize I could play music if I really wanted to.

I soon started to understand just because one person told me I was terrible at something didn't mean it was true! Several years before that, I had fallen in love with an instrument called the hand pan. I loved listening to videos and recordings of this unique and beautiful instrument. It looks a little like a flying saucer and is basically an inverted steel drum. The sound is magical. It's not a common instrument, and in fact, they are somewhat hard to get. I decided I wanted to buy one and learn to actually play an instrument, finally. So what if I was in my late forties. In order to acquire one, I had to get on a waiting list to have one made for me. The company that makes them, at least the one I wanted, was in the Netherlands. It was a couple years' wait, but they would custom make it for me to the scale I chose after listening to recordings of various options.

I picked mine and put my name on the list. Two years later, they contacted me and said they would be making my hand pan next. I was both excited and terrified. It took six more months to get it, and while I still haven't learned it the way I want to (I've been busy writing a book!), I love just playing it and getting comfortable with the way it feels and sounds. I now know I can learn anything I want to. Someone else's idea of what I can and can't do is not real. I've chosen to leave that limiting belief behind me and hand myself over to fully embracing whatever I want to try.

The limiting belief I had no musical talent was based on a story someone else told. This was not my story. I may not be selling seats at concerts or having anyone ask me to play anything, but I no longer believe it's not possible for me to play music if I choose to. I am only held back by the limitations I create in my own mind. It's important to take whatever information we are given and question it. Just think of how many things we may miss out on in life because of a narrative someone else created for us.

Think about everything your life is NOW. What you do, who you spend your time with, your hobbies, your career, your relationships. Imagine you are watching a movie of your life containing these things. How does it make you feel? Are you empowered? Are you happy? Are you satisfied, or are you longing for something else? Maybe not in every category, but are there dreams you have you have not explored, not expressed, or not taken a chance to try?

Now, imagine there is a second movie for you to watch, where all of your wildest dreams play out. The relationship you want, the job, the places you travel to, how you relax, and any other thing you can think of you have not allowed yourself to venture into because of a negative story you've been telling yourself. At the end of this movie, are you energized? Are you excited and confident? Compare the two movies in your mind. Which one would you want to step into given the choice? You are the star of your very own feature film. You are also the writer, director, and producer. Create what you want most.

KEY FOR CHANGE

Exercises to challenge limiting beliefs.

In the last section we identified limiting beliefs you may have, here are the steps to change them.

Think of story you tell yourself or that someone else has told you about yourself that has never felt right for you. Write down what that story is. For example, my story about not being musical. I would write: "I have no musical talent," then you want to challenge the story.

Is this story true? For me...I haven't developed my musical talent yet, but because I want to, it is not a true story. I have not stopped wanting to try, and therefore don't know what is really possible. I'm choosing to challenge that limiting belief and say if and when I am ready, I could have musical ability.

Then ask yourself: "What if it isn't true?" "What could happen if it isn't true?"

Also ask yourself "How do I feel about this story?" You may need to confront those emotions so that you can have a clear picture of the truth. The way to clarity is always in our emotional processing.

Spend some time with your answers and allow yourself to get clear on what you want your new belief to be.

In summary, after you identify your limiting belief, follow these steps:

1. Challenge your limiting belief—ask yourself, Is this true? What if I am wrong? Could I be wrong about this?

2. Question your limiting belief. How is this belief serving me? As with many other negative thought patterns, we will likely have some secondary gain supporting this belief. For example, it might be something like not feeling disappointment if it doesn't work out for you.

3. Create superior alternatives for the limiting belief, by coming up with scenarios and possibilities that go against the belief you held. Imagine what it would be like for the belief to not be true. What does that feel like?

4. Test your alternatives.

Go ahead and try what you have been telling yourself you couldn't do or accomplish and see the positive results you receive.

CHAPTER 17

GROW AND GO

What lies behind us and what lies before us are tiny matters compared to what lies within us

~Henry S. Haskins, *Meditations in Wall Street*

So often we think we are born with the abilities we have, and if they aren't blatantly apparent, then we aren't ever going to be able to expand them. But that is just not true. I always felt creative and artistic; however, when I was younger, what I was able to actually express artistically, if I'm being honest, was not so great. When I went to art school, I started developing my skills and practiced a lot. I found photography which really was my sweet spot. I went on to make handcrafted fine silver jewelry, taught myself different painting techniques, and on and on. I had the feeling of the skill. But I wasn't necessarily naturally good at it. That, I believe, came with time and dedication to making it happen. Yes, some people seem to arrive on earth already being talented in particular areas, but this is not true for everyone. Being able to take our passion for something and practice it to turn it into something more is an example of having a growth mindset.

In 2009, my husband at the time and I decided we were going to move from a Washington, DC, suburb back home to Pennsylvania, and I would be leaving behind my graphic design job with the federal government that I'd had for thirteen years. We wanted me to be able to be home for our sons and be able to take them to their activities, but with the cost of living near Washington, it just wasn't feasible, so moving to an area with a lower cost of living was the only option. I was looking forward to being a stay-at-home mom for a while since I had been working full time with the exception of maternity leave for each of our two sons. Our boys were eight and five by this time. Even though I was excited, I knew I was going to need to find something to do as I enjoy being busy.

One day, I saw a book on making precious metal clay jewelry at a Barnes and Noble and decided right then and there I was going to learn how to do that and go to craft shows to sell what I made. I literally had never tried working with this type of clay medium, but just decided I was going to do it. It sounds so impulsive now as I write this, but it interested me, and I didn't consider I wouldn't be able to do it. While I had a degree in art and had worked in various mediums including pottery throughout my life, I had never really worked with metals and certainly not with this material, which started as clay and when fired in a jeweler's kiln turns into 99.9 percent fine silver as the binder in the clay burns away and the silver particles fuse. I found it to be fascinating and exciting to try something new.

I researched and bought all the tools and supplies including a kiln and clay. I set up a studio space in our new home and then started teaching myself how to create with this new-to-me material. It was a lot of trial and error. I made notes, experimented, read books, and made lots and lots of mistakes while testing everything out. When I think back on that now and realize how I knew absolutely nothing about precious metal clay and invested all that time and money into it anyway, running completely on faith I would be able to figure it out seems a little shocking to me. I believe this way of thinking has served me well as it wasn't the only time I approached a new endeavor this way. It's what having a growth mindset is all about.

When we believe that our abilities, skills, and talents can be developed rather than being innate gifts we are born with, a whole world of possibilities opens up for us. Taking that approach to creating the life we want and the dreams we have will carry us a very long way.

A growth mindset has some distinct characteristics including believing our effort matters, having a knowing our intellectual capacity can be expanded and developed as well as having a desire to seek challenges and opportunities. It's also important to learn how to process difficulties and failures which again goes back to part one of this book. If we are able to work through our feelings when we have things not go well, we are able to maintain a growth mindset and achieve whatever we dream of. Some other benefits to having a growth mindset are adaptability, resiliency, and a positive attitude.

KEY FOR CHANGE

If you are looking at your approach to life or more specifically your goals, do you think you have the characteristics of a growth mindset? If you said yes, that's great, keep going, keep doing what you are doing, letting your world expand and your ceilings be broken through. If you are reading this and feeling like maybe this is an area you might need to make some changes in, consider asking yourself these questions:

Why do I feel like my intelligence and talent are what I have and can't be changed?

How do I deal with setbacks and challenges in my work, hobbies, or relationships?

We can develop a growth mindset in small steps. What are some easy changes you can make today to work toward bigger changes tomorrow?

EXAMPLE: If you want to get healthier but it seems overwhelming, begin today with a fifteen-minute walk. Do that daily for two weeks, soon you'll find yourself wanting to walk longer. Gradually increase the time you walk in small increments until you are walking pre-determined distance or time each day. Add in other small changes along the way like drinking more water or being intentional about how many servings of fruits and vegetables you eat. Soon you will have created an entirely different way of thinking about your health, and you will begin to see results.

Intentional change doesn't happen like an explosion, it happens like a plant grows; from a seed, slowly breaking through the earth, reaching toward the sun.

Some growth mindset characteristics are:

- The belief that Intelligence can be developed and expanded

- Knowing effort matters in mastery of a pursuit

- Having the ability to process failure and find learning in it

- Possessing a positive attitude

- Being resilient

- Having adaptability to adjust to setbacks

- Seeking challenges and taking appropriate risks

CHAPTER 18

WHAT DO YOU WANT?

The great secret of getting what you want from life is to know what you want and believe you can have it.

~ Norman Vincent Peale, *Positive Thinking Every Day*

Once you've realized you are in control of your life, of your choices, and ultimately your experiences, and have adequately faced your fears and any other negative emotions and limiting beliefs that may have been holding you back, it's time to really map out your goals and dreams and make them a reality. I think it's important to get a sense of what you really want, and that clarity will come when you look at how you feel with where you currently are. It will help you see what is working and what isn't and begin to find your way to your happiest self.

All too often we get stuck going round and round doing the same things day after day and not taking a leap into something new. We may find ourself on the treadmill of life for many reasons, but before I get into them, consider a treadmill for a moment. When on a treadmill, our legs keep moving, but we are never really going anywhere. My running friends and I refer to this awful machine as a "dreadmill." We dread getting on it if the weather is bad and it's the only option. So why would we want to put ourselves on a life dreadmill when there are ALWAYS many other options? Sometimes it's self-doubt, sometimes fear, sometimes what we perceive as lack of resources (I say what we perceive, because there are ways to create opportunities we want that may have an initial cost as long as we are committed to finding those ways.) Whether it's a job, a hobby, or a trip around the world, if our dreams combined with dedication are there, we can create the opportunities we desire.

When I decide I want to do something, I tend to throw my entire self into it. I start visualizing what it looks like when I get to the goal. I also try to imagine how it feels to complete this particular thing as well. I look to see who is doing what I want to do and doing it successfully. Then I will try to learn everything I can about the subject. I will get all the tools I need, and then I will start out to do it with a belief I already can. If we believe we are competent and we can do something, the chances are we will. Our mindset plays a critical role in reaching our goals.

Many years ago, my husband at the time and I decided we were going to start a business selling butterflies to release at weddings, funerals, and memorial services. We didn't know anything about butterflies, and I mean, we knew nothing. So, we took a course on how to raise them, how to hatch them, and what to feed them, as well as how to mail them to people.

We built a sunroom on our house to use for this purpose. We went along the highway and cut milkweed plants—the preferred food of monarch caterpillars—and put it in our freezer. We threw ourselves 100 percent into learning everything we could about raising butterflies.

I'd like to say we were incredibly successful at this, but the business didn't take off, no pun intended (ok, maybe it was intended, I love a good pun). I have no regrets over any time we expended learning all we could about butterflies. It taught us many other things. We learned how to follow a process from the ground up, how to get to a goal we wanted to achieve, and also how to know when it was time to let an idea go. To quote Nelson Mandela, "You either win, or you learn." I think that applies to everything, either something takes flight and becomes a fantastic success, or you learn something that will lead you to your great and wild achievement down the road. When I say great and wild achievement, I mean whatever it is that makes you happy. It doesn't mean making millions of dollars, winning awards, or becoming famous, it means being content with how you are using your gifts and the way you spend your days.

Sometimes in life we try things. Sometimes those things sound like a great idea, and even when we've given our best effort, sometimes we just need to let the idea go and allow ourselves to take what we learned and move on. The butterfly business for me was definitely one of those experiences. During the time we were working on that business was when I had my miscarriage, and my priority to have children was much greater to me. Even though I thought the butterfly business was something I wanted to do, my joy was much greater when my son Ben was born, and the butterfly room became a playroom. Don't be afraid to try things, but also don't be afraid to allow yourself to stop trying that thing if it's not lining up with what you really want. It's also important to not get discouraged if something doesn't work out even if it's what you think you really want. It just means these experiences are building blocks for you for your next attempt. Sometimes we have to wash, rinse, repeat until we get to where we were headed all along.

As I talked about in the early chapters, getting emotionally clear will help you determine how you really want to be using your amazing life. It's helpful to set up goals. Begin by deciding what you want to do. Would you like to learn how to cook, mountain climb, write calligraphy, speak Japanese, raise chickens, go back to school for your first degree or your fifth, or maybe you have a great business idea. Whatever it is, decide it. Write it down, tell someone you want to do it. The act of sharing a goal will increase your chances of reaching it, however, be cautious just how much you share it. There are studies that show when we talk about the goal too much, we get wrapped up in the idea of it rather than actually doing the work of it, and our subconscious may begin to believe we've already completed it. Having a few trusted people, like family or close friends who know what you are working on rather than a huge social media announcement until you are closer to the finish line is probably best. In some cases, this is a catch 22 though. For example, if you are like me and have a book writing goal, it's important to have a platform to share it with when you release the book, so I suggest sharing when your project is well underway but not necessarily complete, while still being sure to keep your focus on the desired end results. I shared when I was more than halfway to finishing my book. I was pretty confident at that point that I'd be getting it done soon(ish).

When we don't know how to do something or if something we are doing isn't providing the results we want, we have two options. One is to change course all together, and the second is to try a different approach. This might include getting someone who has more experience at what we are trying to accomplish and use that resource to get us on the right track.

For example, I was struggling with nutrition, so I started to work with a registered dietitian who taught me what my body actually needs. This helped me make positive changes that not only provided the energy I was lacking, but also helped me feel better.

Another example was when I was training for a big race. The training plan I started using wasn't working for me, so I hired a running coach who personalized a program for me and my needs. My performance started to improve. I felt better than ever in a training cycle, recovered faster, and had greater results in the race.

I think we all have blind spots in our lives, and even if we think we are doing everything "right," we might be missing something critical. A second set of eyes is always a good thing. Don't be afraid to look at alternative ways to do things. Chances are someone else out there has more experience than you and can help point you in the right direction.

I understand it might not be in one's budget to hire some-one for everything they need help with, but that's totally ok. There are LOTS of free or very low-cost options out there to help you do almost anything. Just do your research and be sure your source is reputable. As it pertains especially to anything health related, you want to be certain you are not following "fads" but are getting solid, accurate information. Do you want to learn how to paint? How to play guitar? How to dance, sing, or plant a garden? Look online, it's a place where unlimited learning opportunities abound.

The dietitian I had worked with offered paid plans, but she had a lot of free options with the very best and most accu-rate information as well. You can get free or low-cost guidance for whatever it is you want to adjust, change, or learn in your life. It doesn't have to be a big financial risk. See what they offer for free and start there. Sometimes, we can only go so far with our own knowledge, and we need to call in backups. Don't be afraid to ask for help, or to reach out for resources if you are finding yourself stuck.

Once you know what you want to do and have found resources to help you if needed, you have taken a big step. This means you have begun to change your mindset already, going away from what you've always known into new ways of thinking and approaching your dreams. Here are some other helpful ideas for staying focused on and reaching your goals:

Find an accountability partner:

This person can be also working toward a goal, and you can mutually support one another.

Make a vision board:

For some people, having a visual of what it is they are working toward will help them stay focused and committed to reaching it.

Create a mantra:

Having a phrase that keeps you on track can be a good reminder of what it is you really want. An example might be "I am working toward my goal and I'm closer to it every day" or "I always accomplish what I set my mind to."

Layout a plan:

Write a clear plan with steps to take, breaking it down into manageable and attainable pieces. Check in frequently with your plan to see if anything needs to change. Being open to adjustments when needed will keep you from getting stuck.

Speaking of getting stuck…if you find that happening in the process of getting to your end goal, whatever it might be, take some time to circle back to checking in with your feelings. If you feel frozen in your process, try the tapping approach from chapter 2 (also found in more detail on my website: jennifer-riggs.com) and say something like "feeling stuck about_____" (fill in the blank for what it is you are working on). You might find you have a limiting belief or fear that got uncovered in the process. If you address it, you can change your thoughts and move forward again.

For example, you might realize you have a fear of success; which is actually more likely a fear of failure that needs to be confronted. By taking the time to examine and work with the fear, you will make your path clearer.

One day, I was running a fairly challenging trail half marathon, and around mile eleven going for yet another steep climb, I heard someone behind me say, "At least when you fall up, you don't fall as far." It struck me immediately how insightful that was, and my first thought didn't have anything to do with running this race, but rather how this can be true in life. Thinking about staying balanced in our lives and knowing even if we get off track a little, we can find our way back so much easier if we generally try to stay in a moving forward mindset. If we fall on our way up, we might stumble back a few steps, but we can get up and try again.

If you are working toward learning or accomplishing something, and it starts feeling like it doesn't fit you anymore, be sure to check in with your feelings in case it's a negative belief standing in your way. If you've done that and it still doesn't feel right, remember it's ok to change course, sometimes the thing we think we want is really just a doorway to something else. Maybe it was to give you the courage or information for your real goal. Whatever the case might be, always have faith in yourself and your abilities.

In the 1950s, Dr. Curt Richter, a psychology professor at Johns Hopkins, conducted a scientific study where he placed rats in water to see how long they could stay treading above the waterline. For the most part, they gave up after fifteen minutes, and they would sink to the bottom. The researchers would pull them out, allow them to rest a few minutes, and then put them back in the water. How long do you think they were able to tread water the second time?

It was not what I expected, but the results speak to the power of hope and belief in oneself. The rats lasted sixty hours before tiring to exhaustion this time. They didn't give up. They kept their belief in themselves. If rats have the ability to do this, imagine what humans can do. If we stay focused on our goal and keep trying, we will get where we want to go.

KEY FOR CHANGE

- Write down some goals you have.
- Prioritize what you want to accomplish first.
- Ask yourself what you need to reach your goal.
- Make a list of what you need, then research resources to help you attain it.
- Keep your list handy or write on a whiteboard you can easily see daily.

Be sure you are keeping your end goal in sight and write yourself some positive mantras or reminders that you are capable.

It helps to take time to visualize what it looks like when you reach the goal, and also imagine what that *feels* like.

Make notes along the way about what is going well, and what you might want to change or get extra resources for.

Before you know it, you will have accomplished what you set out to.

Some other mindset changes will also help you achieve your goals:

- Challenging negative statements you make about yourself and your goals
- Changing limiting beliefs

CHAPTER 19

ABUNDANCE IS GREATER THAN SCARCITY

True abundance isn't based on our net worth, it's based on our self-worth.

~ Gabrielle Bernstein, *Twitter, August 13, 2012*

We need to create boundaries with our negative thoughts just like we would with people who negatively affect us. It's easy to go down a path of negativity and lack. We begin to doubt ourselves and our abilities to succeed, and therefore, we stop seeing the goodness in our lives. We may believe if there are a lot of people out there doing what we want to do, that door is closed for us. We may believe because we have not had financial wealth up to this point, it will never happen. We may believe we don't have the resources, whether time, money, or education to achieve our dreams. We may believe other people have healthy, happy relationships, but we can't. These are just some examples of scarcity thinking that can sabotage our goals and self-worth.

A scarcity mindset creates the belief there is a limited amount of talent, success, happiness, wealth, love, etc., in the world. This way of thinking has one believing they can't have, do, or be enough. Which ultimately comes from not believing in oneself.

An abundance mindset, on the other hand, creates the belief we live in unlimited possibility, there is enough of everything for everyone, and we are good enough just as we are, and we are worthy of all of the good things life has to offer. When we live in a scarcity mindset, we are so focused on what we don't have it becomes difficult to plan, focus, or make decisions. We end up feeling stressed, anxious, and lonely.

When we live in an abundance mindset, everything in our lives is in harmony, we are able to reach our goals and plan new ones. We feel good, positive, hopeful, and happy. The abundance mindset looks at what is working and going well in life, while the scarcity mindset puts energy into what is not working. When we are in abundance, we feel like we have enough, or even more than enough, but in scarcity, we are always feeling like we are lacking. In abundance, we are embracing change, while in scarcity, we are fearful of change. People who view life through the abundance mindset are always learning while people who are rooted in scarcity feel they already know it all. At first glance, of these qualities, which mindset do you feel you live in? You also may have an abundance mindset in one area of your life, but not in others. For example, you might feel you think abundantly when it comes to finances but are in scarcity about love. We can shift to abundance in all areas; as with any mindset change, it begins with awareness.

Life is not a finite pie only so many slices can come from. It is, in fact, an unlimited buffet! There is more than enough for everyone, and that includes variety and options that are endless. When we focus on what is working, more things begin to work. When we are in that flow, the blessings just keep coming. In fact, when we are in that mindset, we are able to see the blessings in even the not so positive things, because we know we deserve good in our lives, and it will come.

Examples of Abundance vs. Scarcity thinking:

Abundance mindset = What is working
Scarcity mindset = What is not working

Abundance mindset = Thinking Big
Scarcity mindset = Thinking small

Abundance mindset = Plenty
Scarcity mindset = Lack

Abundance mindset = Happiness
Scarcity mindset = Resentment

Abundance mindset = Embracing change
Scarcity mindset = Fear of change

Abundance mindset = Proactive
Scarcity mindset = Reactive

Abundance mindset = Learning
Scarcity mindset = Knowing it all

If you are saying to yourself, "I do look for the blessings and I feel like I'm grateful, but things are still not going the way I would like them to," you may need to circle back to emotional processing. It is once again important for changing your thinking from scarcity to abundance. If you live with a set of beliefs rooted in lack, it is likely something happened in your past that created that belief for you.

I had a client who grew up in poverty. He always had the fear he would be homeless. His parents were averse to working and always put out the "threat" that at any given moment they would lose everything. Therefore, my client grew up fearful this could still be true for them, even though he himself was hardworking and successful. He never quite let himself enjoy the fruits of his labor, believing the rug might be pulled out from under him at any time.

He had to go back to the memories from childhood and process the fear from the moment the announcement his father had lost his job and said he didn't know how long they would have a place to live.

Once he was able to really feel the emotions of that impactful time and connect to his younger self, providing affirmation this story from his past was not true in his present, he began to relax and started enjoying his life and success. He realized he was in control of the experiences he was having, and his hard work and dedication to his goals were what had made this a different outcome from what he had previously believed was possible.

A scarcity mindset isn't only about things related to finances or career success. We can have beliefs that there is a limited amount of happy relationships, achievements in any hobby, sport, or class. We can believe there isn't enough praise, love, or happiness for everyone. It becomes a belief that if you have it, I don't, or vice versa, and so when someone is in scarcity, they will fear competition because they will believe there is a winner and loser in everything, not that there is enough winning to go around.

If you find you are living in a scarcity mindset, begin first by asking yourself, "Why do I feel this way?" "What in my past might have contributed to a fear of not having enough wealth, success, happiness, etc.?" There's probably something from long ago that created a belief for you this is the way it is for you. Remember, we are not ever stuck with any past way of being. You are in control of creating the life you desire, so really put some energy into believing you have more than you ever dreamed of.

KEY FOR CHANGE

Ways to increase (hey, that word even fits this topic!) your abundance mindset

Practice gratitude

If you are noticing a gratitude practice has been suggested before and in other ways, it is because it is a key element to having a positive life. It's difficult to feel negative when we are focusing on what is good in our lives. The more we tune into the good stuff, the less capacity for staying stuck in the bad we have.

Remember the photo gratitude journal I suggested? That would work for this as well, as would a more traditional gratitude journal where you write down a few things each day you are grateful for. If you don't want to take pictures or write things down, just begin to make a habit at the end of your day to say out loud three things you were grateful for that day.

Here are some other things you can do to work toward an abundance mindset.

- Don't be afraid to give. Whether it's your money, time, or talent. When we give sincerely, goodness returns to us. Again, the energy we put out returns to us.

- Celebrate when others, your family, friends, or even strangers succeed. You will not achieve less because someone else wins at something.

- Set BIG goals. If there's something you want to do, imagine you not only do it, but you are the very best there is at it. We can have abundance in self-worth, love, success (whatever that means to you personally), money, time, confidence and more. It's important to not place limitations on whatever it is that you are desiring to create in your life.

- Create abundance affirmations like these to say daily:

  "I am worthy of good things."

  "I am abundant in all areas of my life."

  "I am always good enough."

  "I am creating the life I want."

"I have everything I need to be successful."

"I am aligned with my purpose."

"I believe in myself."

"I am creative and open to new solutions."

"I deserve love and respect."

"I am happy with who I am."

What abundance affirmations can you think of?

CHAPTER 20

Authenticity Guaranteed

Authenticity is the daily practice of letting go of who we think we're supposed to be and embracing who we are.

~ Brene Brown, *The Gifts of Imperfection*

When I was in kindergarten, I was already trying to stretch my creative side. I was a quiet little girl, living in a world in my imagination, envisioning things as I saw them, not necessarily as they were. I remember one day being scolded because we were doing a color by number picture of an Easter egg, and the zigzag lines were to be one color, the ends another, and the middle portions a third color, all defined by the legend on the assignment. I, however, made each zigzag a different color, then each end two other colors, and the middle parts yet another. I remember very distinctly the teacher coming around and looking at my egg, and her look of disapproval was evident. She said, "What are you doing?" And I told her, "Well the colors that we were supposed to use just didn't look right so I made it all these colors instead." I was not praised for that at all, in fact, she was clearly not happy with my use of creativity, because of my lack of ability to follow directions.

Even though that was many, many years ago, that moment was a really defining one in my life. I think it's important to paint your own picture, even if it means being disapproved of, because in the end, you are the only one who needs to approve of you.

What does it mean to be "authentic"?

If you've ever been to New York City, you'll find carts on the street selling Rolex watches, Gucci and Louis Vuitton handbags at unbelievable, rock-bottom prices. Of course, they are such low prices, because they are knock-offs, inauthentic copies of the real deal. If the brand were compared to a personality, being authentic means that your real character and not an act is what you live out of.

The details of who you are, just like the stitching on a bag or the precision mechanisms of a watch, are the most accurate representation of what's inside you and what you display to others.

Sometimes being authentic feels scary. Maybe all the time. We may want to be vulnerable and show our true selves to the world, or at least those around us in our close circle, but the fear of rejection and failure can overpower us and push us back into hiding. That fear is often coupled with shame. Shame makes us feel that we are a bad person, that we are unworthy of being loved and accepted as we are. That we are inherently flawed. In the case of being authentic, shame comes from a feeling that we have gone against our beliefs in an attempt to fit in and be accepted. This can happen un-justly because of ideas that may have gotten into one's mind through negative experiences, usually while still a child. Trauma endured during times of development can make us feel like it's not safe to be ourselves. When we start to let that happen, we may be inclined to shut the door quickly because our subconscious may remember that it wasn't safe before to do that. Oftentimes experiences with neglect, abuse, and dysfunctional relationships can have us feeling like it's wrong to be ourselves.

If you were told through words or actions of another (or many others) that you weren't wanted as you were, the fear of abandonment may keep you wanting to hide your truest self from the world. You may find yourself pretending to be some-one you are not because of the perception that this is what is acceptable. The problem is your subconscious knows the dif-ference between being your true self and copying what feels safe. This is again why processing past emotions is so import-ant. If we can shed the shame, fear, and pain of rejection, we can begin to move into a space of feeling it is ok to be open and authentic with others. We can believe we will be accepted even with our flaws and things that may make us seem "weird" or "different." Something to consider is that if someone doesn't want to be around you because you are being yourself, then they are probably not someone you want to have around you in the first place. We want to surround ourselves with people who love us as we are and encourage our authenticity.

I have asthma, and there's a feeling of relief that comes over my body when I use my inhaler. If I'm having an asthma attack, my throat feels like I can't clear it and taking a breath is difficult. I feel tight and constricted. When I use the inhaler though, there's an intense relief, I can breathe easier, everything in my body relaxes, and I feel calm. It's a stark contrast to the feeling of having your breath taken away. I think this can be compared to what it feels like to be inauthentic. When we are not being true to ourselves, we feel a sense of unrest, tension, and tightness in our body. We may feel almost like we can't exhale. Compare that to situations when we really are being ourselves, as in our close inner circles, or when we are at home with our family. That relaxed peace knowing you can express yourself and be accepted is the best feeling there is.

Being authentic, and true to yourself, are among the most important things. We shouldn't try to make our feet fit our shoes, but rather have our shoes fit our feet. Likewise, we shouldn't make ourselves fit a situation, but rather be accepted as we are. This is especially important in our closest relationships. If you don't feel comfortable with who you are, you'll begin to feel like something is "off." If you are constantly living to fit someone else's idea of what is right for you and you are telling the voice inside yourself to stay quiet, to keep the peace, you'll definitely begin to notice. When we make ourselves small to appease others, we are hurting ourselves deeply.

Don't worry, this is a struggle for lots of people. I think in that process of figuring out who we are and what feels right for us, we can still be authentic as we find our way through the overwhelming information around us. We can own the parts of us that we know in our hearts to be true, and recognize the parts that feel less true, even if we can't take action immediately to change them. We may be in a career that doesn't fit us, or a relationship that feels wrong, but still be able to embrace the pieces of us that DO feel right even though not everything does. If we can offer ourselves some grace as we find our way, it becomes easier to notice when we are acting out of fear and shame and are not being authentic.

Sometimes we have to test things out to see what fits for us.

I went through a time when I decided I didn't want to wear jeans anymore (don't ask me why, I live in them now). I tested out dressing in flowing skirts and blouses or yoga pants and tee shirts with lotus flowers. I also had a phase where I dyed my hair purple for about a year. It was fun to try, but none of these things stuck for me. I definitely have some hippie in my soul, but my outward style has ended up being quite different. What we wear and the interests we have are a part of being our authentic selves, but the core of being authentic is what you believe, your values, and your personality. Trying new outward things can help us understand what inward things are the most real.

The 1961 movie, *Breakfast at Tiffany's* and the 1958 novella of the same name by Truman Capote, whose main character, Holly Golightly, played by Audrey Hepburn, has many themes. The one among them that has always drawn me to call this my favorite movie is that in the story, Holly is struggling to find her true identity. She is masquerading as a party girl hiding her feelings and playing a part in a story that really didn't fit what her heart actually desired. At one point in the movie a character asks someone of Holly, "Is she or ain't she?"

The reply? "Is she or ain't she what?" The response was "a phony." As the story goes on, Holly begins to find her true self. In the end, she discards the outward mask she was hiding behind, and the story she was trying to sell to others. She found a place where she felt loved and accepted as she was.

I think this is what we all ultimately want, to be loved and accepted while expressing our truest selves. To feel that it is safe to show our vulnerabilities and emotions and to let our beliefs and values be known.

Something else to mention about authenticity is that we will of course behave differently in professional situations versus how we are with our friends and then likely even more differently than we will with our family. In each case, we can still be authentic as long as our core beliefs are not compromised. Which means if you value kindness over all else, telling someone the dry cake they made was delicious, you are not being fake, you are being kind, and if kindness is one of your values, then you are being authentic. It all comes down to living out of our beliefs, values, and personality in all situations, even if the response from one person to another is different. For example, we might feel safe to tell our best friend who is going to enter their cake in a contest, that they may want to try a new recipe. The message can be delivered with kindness, but truth can still be shown. The core value of kindness still prevails.

So, what does it mean to be true to yourself? What does it take to make this happen?

Sometimes it's brave action, making choices that feel right even when it's not popular to do so. It's also about honoring your feelings about situations. If you haven't noticed by now, our feelings really matter in all things. The answers are in our subconscious. They are right there in our feelings. Taking time to examine your feelings about any situation will allow you to really be authentic. We need to look at ourselves without all of the protective layers and let ourselves really feel the truth in our hopes and desires.

Some other factors in being true to yourself include not trying to please others at your own expense, and also honoring decisions you make that may go against what others' expectations of you are. You can be true to yourself without malicious intent toward someone else. Which brings me to another point about being authentic. You and you alone are responsible for your actions, just as others are for theirs. If someone disagrees with your choices, that is a place they will need to look inside themselves and examine their feelings. We are also all responsible for our own reactions to others' choices. It's ok to decide what you need and want in your life, and the first real step to authenticity is being honest with yourself about what you want.

Ask yourself what do I want and what is best for me? Not what "should" I do.

The word "should" creates judgement when we say it to others, but equally so when we say it to ourselves. If we say we "should" keep this job, or be involved in an activity that we don't enjoy, we are keeping ourselves from healthy feelings of authenticity. It's like setting a trap for yourself. You might fall in the hole and see the light at the top, but find yourself trying to climb out and having the walls of the hole crumble around you. There's not much to grab onto when we are pretending.

Sometimes we feel authentic, while other times we don't, but if we are generally trying to be our most real selves and have an awareness of when we are not, we are going to feel happier. Positive things will happen when you really get in touch with your own heart. You will have a feeling of freedom, confidence in yourself and your decisions, as well as a greater sense of self-worth.

 ## KEY FOR CHANGE

Exercise in authenticity.

Grab a pen and paper and answer the following questions:

- Where do you feel the most happy?

- Where do you feel the most relaxed?

- What things do you participate in that go against your values and beliefs? What things do you participate in that are in alignment with them?

- Are you satisfied with your job? If not, what would you rather do?

- What is your ideal way to spend free time? How often do you get to do that?

- Are there things you want to say to people in your life but avoid so you don't rock the boat? If so, who are those people and what are the things you want to say (this is not a license to be mean or rude, it is meant as a way to be honest about yourself, not cast judgment on others).

- Are you happy with your relationships with your family, your spouse, and your friends? If there is one or more that upset you regularly, you may need to address issues with that person head on to resolve problems. You may need to create boundaries. There also may be emotions you need to process that could be inhibiting either improving or changing those relationships.

- What dreams do you have for the future?

Once you've answered these questions, begin assessing how much of your actual life lines up with your answers. Then you can start making changes that match up with the truth of who you are.

You've Got Personality

Understand yourself and you'll understand others better too.

When it comes to being authentic, it helps if we can really understand our personality. When I began to learn more about my personality type and why I do the things I do, life got easier. When I started realizing there were very distinct reasons why I behave the way I do in different situations, I could see where at times I was feeling hurt because others may not have seen things the way I did. It opened my eyes to realize this is a big world and we all have our unique way of looking at things. That being said, there are a certain number of personality types, and understanding your type can really take some of the mystery out of what you do and why you do it.

If you've never done a personality test, it might be a fun thing for you to try. If you can get your spouse, partner, friends, family, and/or coworkers to do one also, you may find you can help heal some things in your relationships as well as within yourself, in addition to improving communication. Yes, we do things because of experiences we have had, but we also have innate qualities that direct our behaviors as well.

If we don't understand ourselves or those we interact with, it's kind of like trying to assemble a puzzle without the box with the picture. You'll have all these random pieces, and no idea of what to do with them. Things become much clearer when we have insight into our behaviors, preferences, and unique qualities. Some personality types are less common than others as well, and if you find yourself feeling like the "odd man out" in situations, this may be why. You may have a less common personality type. It can help you to see your uniqueness as a blessing rather than a challenge.

The more we know ourselves, the more authentic we can be. Authenticity brings inner peace and loving acceptance of ourselves as well as others.

KEY FOR CHANGE

Try taking a personality test. My favorite is Meyers Briggs, and you can find a free test online at **16personalities.com**.

You Always Know

Have you ever had a bad feeling about something, and then later recalled that feeling after the situation may not have played out well? Have you asked yourself, "Why didn't I listen to that feeling I had?" I'm sure you've heard countless stories of people who had an uncomfortable sense about something and changed plans at the last minute or drove a different route to work only to find out there was a terrible accident on their regular route at the exact time they would normally be there. Their intuition let them know something was not right with what they were about to do. Intuition can come into play for the big things in life such as avoiding an accident or making financial decisions, but it happens in small ways in our lives too. In any case, all of the internal guidance we receive is valuable. We need to learn how to decipher it and when we should and shouldn't take action. Trusting your intuition will help you make choices that lead you to your most authentic self.

I was recently talking with a woman at a networking group and the topic of intuition came up. She shared a story from when she was in her early twenties. She was living in a small apartment in a big city. One day she went to open her door and she felt like there was an invisible wall stopping her from entering. She realized a light she had left on was now off. She reasoned that it could have burned out and tried to make herself walk in, but the overwhelming feeling that she shouldn't, hit her hard.

She walked back down to the street and called a friend as well as the police. When the authorities arrived, they all entered the apartment to find disarray in her bedroom. Items thrown on the floor and turned over. Nothing was missing, but someone had clearly been there. At that time there had been a serial rapist in the city. He was later apprehended, and it turned out he lived nearby and indeed had been in her room, waiting to attack her.

It's moments like this we especially need to follow that inner guidance we have. The more in tune we are to our subconscious, the more aware we will be when those warnings go up for us. It's an internal protection system.

Once not too long ago, my husband and two sons and I were heading to a restaurant for dinner. This particular restaurant was situated on a golf course. As we approached the entrance to the restaurant, we saw police cars and quickly determined there had been an accident. They subsequently closed the entry to the parking lot. We went down another road and circled back to park in a lot of another nearby business. My husband said we could just walk across a small section of the golf course until we came to the golf cart path and walk to dinner that way. I said, "That's not a good idea," he said, "It's fine, nothing is going to happen," but I felt in my gut we should walk down the road instead and go around to the front entrance. I repeated several times we shouldn't do it. My sons also chimed in with "It's ok, nothing will happen, Mom." I relented feeling outnumbered. We walked across the section of green grass until we came to the paved path. I tried to keep everyone walking as quickly as possible until we reached the parking lot. Sure enough, as they all said, it was totally fine. We went in and had a nice dinner on the outdoor terrace overlooking the golf course and the soon-to-be-setting sun.

As we got up to leave, I again reminded everyone to be careful walking back to the car. They all laughed at me as we started the trek back to where we had parked. My husband was a few steps ahead of me when suddenly I saw him jerk quickly to the left and heard him yell "Look out!" just as I felt the intense smack into my upper leg. I was confused for a moment and then realized as I felt the sting growing and saw the hard, white ball bouncing a few feet away that as I predicted, walking on the golf course was indeed a poor idea! Thankfully, I only received a pretty substantial bruise, but it could have been much worse. My husband said it whooshed past his face, and had he not quickly moved his head to the left, it would have hit him near his eye. My intuition told me the path we took was not a safe one, but we didn't listen. I think if I was alone, I would have gone the long way around, but because everyone else thought I was overreacting, I gave in. I do think we need to remember to hear our guidance and listen even when it seems unpopular to do so.

Another time I didn't follow my gut on a situation, I ended up with an injury. Some of my running friends were signing up to run the Marine Corps Marathon, and I thought, "I'll do it too." I had run that particular marathon thirteen years before as my very first marathon, and I didn't do as well there as I had hoped, so I decided I'd give it another try. The day the registration opened I had an uneasy feeling about it. I kept telling myself I was just being silly, I had a bad memory of the other time I had run it, and that's probably what I was feeling. Most big races sell out quite quickly, and so you usually want to sign up right when they open, but I didn't do it. I kept feeling uneasy, but also was feeling like I'd feel left out when the race day came if I didn't sign up.

The registration day was also the day my son Nick was graduating from high school, and so I was busy with family visiting and going to the ceremony and party following the graduation. I told myself if they still had spots that night when I returned home, I would then sign up, but in my heart, I was hoping it would be full because I felt so "off" about the whole thing. I didn't have a real reason to not do it, just that gut feeling. Before I went to bed that night, I checked the website and found, quite surprisingly, it still had spots open for registration. The uneasy feeling remained, but eventually, I talked myself into signing up. I thought I'd be relieved after I did, but the feeling didn't go away. I didn't even tell my friends who were going to do the race I had signed up until two weeks later.

A few months passed, and it was time to start training. In marathon training plans you have a gradual increase in weekly mileage with a few low to mid-range distances on weekdays and a "long run" on the weekends. Most schedules take you up to a distance of twenty miles for your long run before you "taper" and gradually decrease for a couple weeks before the race. So, you'd run seventeen miles one Saturday, then eighteen the next, and so on. About halfway through the training cycle, I started to have a nagging pain in my lower leg. I kept thinking it was shin splints, but it was just on one leg, and nothing seemed to help it. It got a little worse each week, and finally after I'd reached the nineteen-mile week, I decided to go have it looked at by a doctor. I unfortunately had developed a stress fracture and wouldn't be able to run for six weeks. My training and marathon ended there. If only

I had listened to that little feeling I had, I might not have had this happen. Thankfully, in my two personal examples, ignoring my intuition had reasonably minor consequences, but what about the woman in the first story I shared? If she had ignored the feeling she had, it could have been catastrophic for her.

The problem is sometimes we think our intuition should be telling us "exactly" what will happen or we should do, but it doesn't work that way. Sometimes we will just get nudges from feelings we have. Though sometimes it comes in louder and stronger than that, as with the woman feeling an invisible wall stopping her from entering her apartment. I think we need to learn to hear both the shouts and the whispers.

My husband Mark is allergic to bees, and he generally will do anything to avoid them, but surprisingly will often drive with his car windows down on warm days. Once he was driving on the highway with his windows wide open, and he said he literally heard a voice from the back seat say, "How about it you put that window up?" He said he was confused and stunned since he was driving alone. After a quick glance in his back seat and confirming there was no one there, he decided he would listen to the voice and put the window up. Seconds later, a swarm of yellow jackets pelted the side of his car. If he'd had the window down, they would have flown directly into him. In this case, the small, quiet voice was a loud, urging shout.

Wouldn't it be nice if all of our intuition moments came out as clearly as the "put the window up" command, or the invisible energetic wall? Of course, it would be, but since that is not how most of them happen, we need to learn to dial into our whispers too. When interacting with someone, do you feel uneasy? Does it feel like you can't take a deep breath in their presence? Do you get a sick feeling at the thought of something you are unsure of? (This one can be especially confusing, since sometimes the "off feeling" we get is just fear because something is unknown or different.) I do feel like there are subtle cues we can learn that tell us when we are just scared because we don't know something, and when we feel "off" because something is truly not a good idea. You can practice differentiating the two by once again closing your eyes and asking yourself some questions, such as "Am I afraid because this is unknown?" or "Is there something I am missing in this situation?"

I think this comes from practice and paying attention to what we experience and making mental notes about how things feel and how they end up turning out. It gives us a reference point for future events.

So, why is intuition even a topic in this book about processing your feelings, changing mindsets, and finding your true self? Well, when we listen to our internal dialogue, we are learning how to trust ourselves, and trusting ourselves is paramount to being true to ourselves. We want to trust our decisions and our path, and on the journey to getting to our destination of meeting ourselves, we need to follow our own advice and guidance.

It's also important to learn to discern gut feelings or intuition from fear. Fear will try to trick us and make us feel something isn't safe when really, we are just not acknowledging our fears. Refer back to the chapter on fear to be sure and process your worries about situations so that you can hear and follow your inner guidance with ease.

We have this little robot vacuum that cleans our swimming pool. You drop the machine into the water, and it runs a cycle scooting around the bottom and up the walls of the pool, cleaning as it goes. When it's done, there's a button to push that tells it to go up the nearest wall, so you can pull it out. One day, I went to retrieve it and was happy to see it had come to rest at the side of the pool nearest the little shed where we keep it. "Oh good," I thought. "Now I don't have to carry it all the way around the pool." I pushed the button, and to my dismay, watched the thing leave its nearby spot and roll to the furthest corner of the pool and slowly came to the surface. I was confused. It was right here…why did it go so far out of its way? As I pulled it from the water, I was thinking about how we do this too. Sometimes the answers are right in front of us, but instead of making it easy on ourselves, we go out of our way to make things harder than they need to be. We need to learn to trust our instincts, abilities, and know things don't always have to follow the most difficult path, just the path that feels the truest to us.

🔑 KEY FOR CHANGE

As with many of my suggestions for positive change, you can sit quietly taking some deep, complete breaths, then think about a situation you would like some guidance on. Really try to focus on the problem at hand for a few minutes.

Ask your subconscious to reveal to you the best solution for you. Then just take a few more breaths and resume your day knowing your answer will come to you. Be sure to pay attention to any feelings or thoughts that arise in the next few days about your question.

CHAPTER 21

Conclusion

Healing is a constant journey, a continual work in progress that has value in every experience. I used to think I would somehow magically find the answer to every struggle in my life and then suddenly wouldn't have to go through any more difficulties. The truth is though, it's a lifelong process, and while we can attain peace and solid positive changes, there's never really a completion as long as we are walking this earth. We will always need to do some sort of "maintenance." This is actually a beautiful thing. The more I learn about myself, the deeper my understanding of others grows too, but I'm always learning, always changing. We all are.

I recently finished a two-and half-year process of having Invisalign on my teeth. I think the healing process is a lot like this. I had for all my life been self-conscious of my teeth. I had some significant spacing on one side and would be careful to turn my head just so for photos or when talking to someone new.

One day, I decided I wanted to correct that. I had gotten to the point where it felt important to me to change this. I wanted to feel confident when I smiled. The idea of having braces in my late forties was not one I relished, but I was excited at the prospect of a brand-new smile. Invisalign seemed like a good solution. They were not terribly noticeable by others, and while they were sometimes uncomfortable, and kind of inconvenient, I felt like it was worth the result I would be getting.

The changes took time, sometimes it seemed like way too long, and I felt impatient. The changes were small, almost imperceptible. Tiny movement of teeth that needed to shift and turn. Sometimes, it wasn't bad, but other times, I felt like I would never be done and would forever be thinking about how I wished I could eat something while not having to deal with this annoyance. At one point, I thought for sure I was going to be done early because everything looked lined up nicely to me, but when I visited my orthodontist, they told me my bite still needed adjusting. I thought this was crazy, I couldn't even see that. Everything looked fine! So, I dutifully started another set of trays, changing them each week so that the next set of subtle movements could happen. Then, finally the day came I was supposed to be done with them, and I felt disappointed because after the bite adjustments, I felt like there were some new spaces opened up that were not there before. I felt confused and frustrated after all this time I was going to be done, but I didn't like what I saw.

The orthodontist told me we could do another set of trays, and so I agreed, and after another three months, the real finish date finally came. I did a two-week whitening process, and also had a few teeth bonded to change the shape to fit the rest of the teeth better. So many steps, so many stages, but here I was, with a new, improved, and beautiful smile I was in love with! It was amazing to me after all those years of disliking my teeth, I could just decide I wanted to change them. Yes, the process was somewhat uncomfortable, it was slow, it often seemed like nothing was happening, but in the end, all of those tiny steps and parts led to a great reward.

Then they fitted me for retainers which I need to wear nightly for the rest of my life to keep my smile lined up as it is now. I think this is so apropos to comparing this whole experience to emotional healing. I had to find myself in a place where I was unhappy enough with something to change it. I had to endure the uncomfortable times. I had to be patient and sometimes it seemed like it was one step forward and two steps back, but things were happening, and I was feeling better about it. Then when it was all said and done, I realized I needed to do maintenance to keep things the way I wanted them to be.

Yes, just like healing. When we are uncomfortable enough, we will make changes, and if we want to keep those changes, we will do what is necessary to make sure we are not falling into old ways. I believe this includes a practice of consistent emotional processing. The more dedicated we are to something we feel is important, the better our long-term results will be. I fully intend to not only keep my smile aligned, but my mind, body, and spirit as well. My hope for you is you will find the tapestry of stages and steps that bring you that same heart conscious alignment in your life.

As I was writing this book, it became more and more

apparent the concepts within were woven together and sometimes were tangled up, because that's how healing itself is. It's not a straight path. There are right turns and left turns and upside-down turns, and sometimes spin in circles until you are dizzy and throw up turns. Sometimes you think you've passed a particular landmark only to find you need to circle back and visit it again. And you know what? That's ok. Healing is messy and complicated and so very beautiful at the same time. As each layer of pain and confusion is stripped away, the truth becomes clearer, and the feeling of peace that sets into the soul is both undeniable and irreplaceable.

While I've written individual chapters and topics, there's usually more than one thing going on in a particular issue, so sometimes we get a "two-fer" and resolve or shift more than one thing at a time, and who doesn't like a great deal? As my grandmother Maggie used to say, when clipping coupons or finding a fantastic sale, "You can't beat that!"

If we take the time to connect with our subconscious mind, our hopes, our joys, our sorrows, and fears, and give them all a voice, our body, mind, and spirit will all benefit in positive and profound ways. The way to freedom and to be our truest self is by letting our feelings be expressed and understood. When we clear the negative cognitions and feelings, the sense of overwhelm we so often carry will diminish as we make the way available to create and carry out new and better ways of living our lives. That happiness is not a mere dream, but our truest reality.

When we heal ourselves, we in turn heal the world. Every person healed heals us all. Every bit of healing done works together in a collective effort to change us all, and that is a truly beautiful thing. May the door to your cage not only be open, but may the bars fall away completely and may the freedom you desire and deserve truly be yours now and forever.

ACKNOWLEDGEMENTS

With deep gratitude for my family, including my husband Mark, and my sons, Ben and Nick for their patience and understanding, as I worked long hours on this book as well as providing feedback again and again. I couldn't have done this without you. Your suggestions, ideas, and most of all, love and support mean the world to me. I love you all.

To my mom, Debbie and step dad, John, for providing stability and love as well as instilling in me the qualities of good work ethic and drive and the knowing that I can do whatever I set my mind to.

To my brother, James who willingly talked about hard things whenever I needed him to, and for always being one of my biggest cheerleaders.

To my running friends, too many to list entirely, whom while on the road or trails I shared my ideas and asked questions to as I found inspiration in our interactions which made its way to these pages. We are more than friends, we are soul/sole sisters.

To my hypnotherapy mentor and friend, Randy Shaw who taught me so much about understanding the power of the subconscious mind and more, and without whom my own personal healing wouldn't have happened to this point.

To Dayna Merryman M.Div., LCSW—Thank you for

your thoughtful review and feedback on the content of my book. Your insight and knowledge helped me more than you know.

To my clients, who have trusted me and allowed me to join them on their healing journeys, I, too, have healed parts of myself in every one of your sessions. I've cried and celebrated with every one of you.

To Richard Paul Evans, I have learned so much from your wisdom and guidance through your Author Ready program. I'm grateful for you and the family of writers you have created and all of the friendships I've made in this process. For anyone who wants to write a book, there's a wealth of information at: authorready.com

With gratitude to Kim Autry, my copy editor for her attention to detail, and expertise in fine tuning my words, to Francine Platt of Eden Graphics, for her talent and patience in designing a beautiful layout for my book, and to Klassic Designs for creating my cover artwork, I couldn't be happier with the results of your contributions and how it all came together.

A big thank you to Marc Roberge and the band O.A.R. for allowing me to quote their song, *I Go Through*. If you haven't heard the song, I highly recommend it, and all of their music.

ABOUT THE AUTHOR

JENNIFER RIGGS is a certified Hypnotherapist and Mindset Coach who is passionate about helping people release their negative emotions to discover their true selves and lead a happier life. She has been working with clients in a healing capacity for over a decade and wants to share the wisdom and understanding of self and others that this work has and continues to teach her.

Jennifer's other interests include photography, painting, distance running, time in nature, reading, and being with family and friends. She lives near Gettysburg, Pennsylvania, with her husband Mark, sons Ben and Nick and their dog, Echo. To learn more about Jennifer and the work she does, visit her website at **Jennifer-Riggs.com**

www.ingramcontent.com/pod-product-compliance
Lightning Source LLC
Chambersburg PA
CBHW051302120626
46547CB00015B/2050